MW01297098

HILLARY CLINTON NUDE

Naked Ambition, Hillary Clinton And America's Demise

by

Sheldon Filger

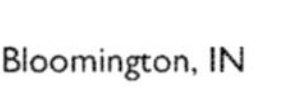
Bloomington, IN

Milton Keynes, UK

AuthorHouse™
1663 Liberty Drive, Suite 200
Bloomington, IN 47403
www.authorhouse.com
Phone: 1-800-839-8640

AuthorHouse™ UK Ltd.
500 Avebury Boulevard
Central Milton Keynes, MK9 2BE
www.authorhouse.co.uk
Phone: 08001974150

First published by AuthorHouse 10/6/2006

ISBN: 1-4259-6759-0 (sc)

Printed in the United States of America
Bloomington, Indiana

This book is printed on acid-free paper.

Cover Design by Molly Crabapple

TABLE OF CONTENTS

Introduction vii

The Yale Mafia 1

A Terminally Unethical and Vulgar Couple 9

Carpetbagger Senator 33

Between Iraq and a Hard Place 47

Celebrity Politics, Imagery and Dynastic Rule 77

Hundred Thousand Dollar Lady 97

Hillary Clinton's Intellect 113

Mediocrity Triumphant 127

Goddess of War 145

America's Clintonian Nightmare 183

INTRODUCTION

Love of power, operating through greed and through personal ambition, was the cause of all these evils.

Thucydides, from *History Of The Peloponnesian War*

Hillary Clinton is far from unique as an American political phenomenon. In most respects, she is in harmony with many other politicians in the United States who have ambitions fueled by insatiable egos. Her flaws and vices are not distinct from what is all too common among many individuals who comprise the American political establishment. And therein lies the danger of her election as the 44th president of the United States.

At a time of immense criticality, America urgently requires excellence in leadership. Unfortunately, the political horizon is thickly shrouded with mediocre pretenders to the throne. Hillary Clinton is already being proclaimed as a front-runner for succeeding the inept

George W. Bush. She personifies the worst of what is being offered to the American people by their broken and dangerously flawed political system. Far from being a superlative figure of state, her unexceptional character only made remarkable by grandiose personal ambition will ensure that America lacks the leadership skills and qualities that are imperative for her to endure as the world's major power. A second Clinton presidency, personified by the megalomaniac carpetbagger senator from New York, will put finality to the accelerating path to national ruin that the United States is currently embarked upon.

"Hillary Clinton Nude" seeks to strip bare the propaganda and PR spin that her campaign directors and consultants will inevitably cook up in the 2008 presidential campaign. What will remain is raw naked truth. However, this book goes beyond exposing Hillary Clinton. She is a microcosm of all that is rotten and insufferable about the American political system in its current state of deformity. Observing Hillary Clinton "nude" will almost blind us by the light of painful truth, for to understand what is nightmarish about the prospects of her presidency, one must also comprehend what has become terminally corroded within the wider political culture and social context that has given birth to America's present state of distress.

THE YALE MAFIA

In virtually every city and town in the United States of America, there exists an elite club or association that is known to the locals as the "in" place to belong. That is, if you want that lucrative government contract, or heads-up on a big sales opportunity with the largest franchise, or inside-information on a multi-million dollar business deal. In their collective cynicism, the American people have become accustomed to the understanding that the most important opportunities in the nation benefiting individuals occur not due to merit but rather "networking" and inside connections.

Suppose there was one such elite club that was so well connected, it had the power to select all the recent occupants of the White House. Sounds too conspiratorial to be true, right? Well, guess again.

The last three American presidents are all graduates of Yale University. Should George W. Bush serve out his entire second term, this would mean that he, his father and William Jefferson Clinton have collectively presided over the White House for a combined total of 20 years.

Hillary Rodham Clinton is also a product of Yale. It was as a student at Yale's law school that she met her future husband, fellow aspiring attorney William Clinton. If she is elected president and serves two terms, this would mean that America would have been under the uninterrupted tutelage of the Yale Alumnus for a total of 28 years!

There are over 3,500 colleges and universities in the United States. Of all these many and varied institutions of higher leaning, what is it about Hillary Clinton's graduate alma mater that renders Yale so unique and exceptional that it alone should have been the school of choice for the men and possibly woman who would rule the United States as chief executive and commander-in-chief for almost a third of a century, without interruption?

On the surface, there would appear to be nothing exceptional. However, when one delves into the 300-year-old history of this sanctimonious institution, one is confronted with some disquieting truths. During the early history of Yale, slave trading was an indispensable resource contributing to its establishment and growth. The first scholarships and endowed professorships at Yale were the product of slave trading money. The library endowment was first established from contributions made by lucrative slave traders. Some of the names of these traffickers in human bondage were carved into the tower in the center of the Yale campus as "Worthies" as recently as forty years ago.

Viewed dispassionately and objectively, one must conclude that there is nothing uniquely special about the moral qualities of the revered institution nestled within the decrepit urban confines of New Haven as an anomaly of affluence.

The other question that may arise is if the intellectual prowess of Yale, if not its moral antecedents, grant it such lofty superiority, it can justify itself as the "required" school for all aspiring American presidents.

There is no factual basis to make such broad assertions regarding Yale's superiority. By virtue of its long history and status as an Ivy League school, it has built up a vast endowment, courtesy of its wealthy alumni basis and the school's aggressive fundraising. Such resources have enabled Yale to recruit well-published and highly recognized faculty from a number of disciplines, as have other Ivy League schools. However, notwithstanding Yale's excellence in a number of academic specialties, it is clearly not overwhelmingly superior to America's 3,500 other colleges and universities to an extent that would logically explain why this one university has monopolized the Oval Office in the White House to such a staggering extent. In fact, in an age of high technology, there are many universities across the United States that are vastly superior to Yale's performance in creating research and skilled alumni to spearhead the information age.

Shorn of its mythology and viewed within a strictly factual context, it must be clear to any sober-minded person that Yale University is not so massively outstanding and celestial an institution in comparison with the nation's other institutions of higher learning. This sobering observation begs the question: why has the White House been monopolized for five consecutive terms by Yale Alumni, from both the undergraduate and graduate level, which possibly rises to seven terms with a President Hillary Clinton?

Since no objective person can conclude, based on the factual record, that Yale is a citadel of vastly superior higher education in comparison with 3,500 other colleges and universities to an extent that justifies its stranglehold on the presidency, perhaps this outcome is a matter of simple coincidence?

There is no mathematical logarithm or formula this writer is cognizant of that could explain, even superficially, such a remarkable record of grooming leaders for the highest office in the land. Perhaps the odds of such an occurrence happening through natural coincidence can be calculated or deduced. In all probability, we would be looking at an astronomical equation, perhaps on the order of billions or trillions to one, that it is only a freakish coincidence which explains why up to seven consecutive presidential terms of office have been served by the products of the garnished halls of Yale University.

If logic alone provides no rational explanation for Yale University's remarkable record of "owning" the White House, could there be a conspiratorial explanation? Though some may point to the secretive "Skull and Bones" fraternity at Yale, of which both George Bush senior and his son, G.W. Bush, have been members, as suggestive of dark forces in New Haven being the hidden wire-pullers of American politics, perhaps the truth is more basic.

In this writer's opinion, American politics have been so severely degraded, it is inconceivable in contemporary America that occupancy can be claimed in the White House solely through meritorious service. Having one academic institution out of more than 3,500 monopolizing the White House for possibly three consecutive decades offers perhaps the most poignant commentary on how dysfunctional America's political structures have become. The presidential candidacy of Hillary Clinton must be viewed from this prism.

A powerful clique that monopolizes illegal and profitable business enterprises is known as a Mafia. However, Mafia is a very appropriate terminology in describing a powerful political elite that bases its stranglehold on power on corruption, lies and sordid infusions of tainted money.

Since the inauguration of William Jefferson Clinton, Yale-trained lawyer, as the 42nd American president in January, 1993 the American people in their cynical common-sense have become accustomed to national leaders who are proven liars, deceivers and con-artists, in alliance with other tainted politicians, all nourished by money provided by the unscrupulous manipulators of the American political system. Perhaps there was a time in America when the character of the president did not have a decisive impact on the welfare of the American republic. Unfortunately, to paraphrase Bob Dylan, the "times are a changing."

In the early part of the twenty-first century, the forces of financial globalism, international terrorism, environmental degradation and nuclear proliferation are converging at a rate that spells catastrophe for America, and indeed the entire planet. To a large extent, all these negative trends can be accelerated or attenuated based largely on the caliber and character of the president of the United States of America. Unfortunately, the corrupt state of American politics does not augur well for the choices available to the American electorate in the upcoming presidential election.

With two consecutive members of the Yale Mafia already proven to be dangerously inept presidents, irrespective of party affiliation, one would think that offering another Yale alum as the "front-runner" in the next presidential election is a grotesque display of bad humor on the part of the wire-pullers who dominate American politics through behind-the-scenes financial support, in exchange for access and favors that satisfy the most narrow definition of selfishness. However, there is nothing funny in what is occurring in contemporary American politics.

The current masters of American politics are not the least interested in merit and openness as the determinants of whom is the leading contender for the White House. They wish to perpetuate a system that is ruinous beyond comprehension, as long as a very small clique of beneficiaries continues to be satiated by their dominance. Keeping the Yale Mafia in charge is the most compelling assurance the backers of America's political morass can obtain that their lucrative and deceitful mastery will be maintained.

The Yale connection is not the sole explanation for the deplorable menu of political options offered to the subjugated American people. However, this disturbing element in the control of the White House for a period of decades serves as an enlightening metaphor for the many other aspects of decay that characterize American politics. In exploring further why Yale law school graduate Hillary Clinton will only further exacerbate the catastrophic trend in American politics, we must peer into her connection with that other product of Yale's august legal training, her life-long partner, President William Jefferson Clinton.

A TERMINALLY UNETHICAL AND VULGAR COUPLE

On paper, Bill Clinton's Vice President, Al Gore, should have been a certainty to succeed him. Theoretically, the American economy seemed uncharacteristically robust. After a long period of federal budget deficits, revenue was at last exceeding governmental expenditures. Budget surpluses were supposedly assured for the future, and unemployment was at a historically low level.

Yet, despite favorable circumstances, the power of incumbency and even garnering more than half a million votes above what his opponent achieved in the November, 2000 presidential election, Gore still lost to George W. Bush. His defeat in part was attributable to America's antiquated College of Electors system, which can (and did) nullify the popular vote, as well as questionable voting in Florida and the unprecedented role of the Supreme Court in ruling against a recount of the controversial Florida vote. Despite all these elements, it must also be recognized that Bill Clinton had garnered such a loathsome reputation for sleazy behavior among large segments of the American electorate, many Americans overlooked what they perceived to be a positive economic climate in selecting Gore's opponent, George W. Bush, who ran on a platform of "restoring honor" to the White House. As bizarre as it may seem in retrospect, millions of Americans, notwithstanding their other uncertainties regarding the intellectual capacity of George W. Bush, accepted the claims made by the Bush campaign that Gores's opponent was a man of integrity, truthfulness and honor.

It is always challenging to recapture the essence of a presidential era, as time serves to mollify the extremities of egregious behavior by politicians. However, an objective journey into the presidency of Bill Clinton helps restore clarity into the degree of White House sleaziness that so appalled American voters when they had to make their selection in November of 2000. Gore paid the price for the disgust that Clinton aroused in many Americans. In a macabre juxtaposition, as Gore went down in flames, Hillary Clinton had just successfully passed her first benchmark on the road back into the White House, by becoming a first among First Ladies in winning election as the senator from New York.

In assessing Hillary Clinton, we cannot dichotomize her from the reputation that Bill Clinton created for himself as president. In recalling the sleaziness of the Clinton White House, the journey should begin at the end of his term, the very last days in office. The decisions he made during those days, and the manner in which they were executed, say more about the amorality and distorted ethos of the Clinton administration than all the other scandals weighed cumulatively.

Marc Rich, an international commodities trader who accumulated vast wealth said to be in the billions of dollars, fled the United States for Switzerland in 1983 to escape criminal prosecution. The charges he faced were of a very serious nature: tax evasion and illegally conducting oil deals with Iran, this in relation to the Iranian government's seizing the American embassy and holding its diplomats hostage for 444 days.

On Clinton's last day in office, he rushed through a series of presidential pardons. While the constitution does grant the president the right to grant clemency to an individual convicted of, or charged with a crime, traditionally this power has been exercised with a degree of constraint, or for reasons claimed to be in the public interest. For example, when President Ford pardoned his predecessor, Richard Nixon, in connection with possible crimes connected with the Watergate scandal, the action did arouse controversy. Yet, most would agree that Ford's motivation was based on sparing the American people further trauma deriving from the Watergate affair. However, Clinton's use of his prerogatives for granting presidential pardons seemed based on a rationale from another universe.

After being a fugitive from American justice for seventeen years, Marc Rich the billionaire was granted a complete pardon by Bill Clinton, literally in the waning hours of his administration. Considering that Mr. Rich had once been on the FBI's list of ten most wanted fugitives, this was a surprising act of beneficence, to say the least. Yet, as shocking as this bizarre act of presidential clemency appeared on the surface, it would soon be clear that there was much more to the Marc Rich affair than met the eye, at least on first impression.

It soon transpired that a strange coterie of "friends" of Rich had been lobbying President Clinton. One of the interlocutors was Denise Rich, ex-wife of the billionaire who still kept on good terms with her fugitive former husband. And what were the connections Denise Rich had to the Clintons? She was a major fund-raiser for the Democratic Party, and contributor for the planned Clinton Presidential Library. Other persons representing interests that had received large financial contributions from Marc Rich, including a former Israeli Prime Minister and a leader of a major Jewish non-profit organization approached Bill Clinton on behalf of the fugitive.

There was also Marc Rich's attorney, Jack Quinn. Mr. Quinn was an astute choice. As it transpired, Jack Quinn was a former White House Counsel during the Clinton administration, retaining excellent access to his former "client." Illustrative of Quinn's influence on

Bill Clinton was the president's lame explanation for the pardon, claiming that Quinn had made "a very compelling case."

Anticipating the outrage of federal prosecutors, Mr. Clinton kept his plans for pardoning Marc Rich top secret, until literally his final hours as president.

The normal procedure for handling presidential pardons is for applications to be submitted to the Justice Department, which carefully vets them before submitting recommendations for the president to consider. With the Clintons, this process was thrown out the window, as an outrageous usurpation of presidential prerogative was stealthily meandered though the dark confines of a corrupted White House.

It soon transpired that the case of Marc Rich was only one of a whole host of questionable last-minute presidential pardons granted by the soon-to-be ex-president. Perhaps one other example displays even more political cynicism. Consider the case of the four men from New Square, in the State of New York.

New Square is a Hassidic enclave in Rockland County, located beyond the New York City metropolitan area. Its demographics include the peculiar statistic that virtually every family in the enclave receives some form of federal monetary assistance. After an investigation by the United States attorney for the region, six men were indicted for devising a complex scheme to defraud the federal government of tens of millions of dollars. These funds were intended for low-income citizens, and the well-organized embezzlement program, which included the establishment of phony schools, involved leaders of the community, including one of its founders. Initially, two of the indicted men fled the country, while four others were convicted and sentenced to prison. Then came Hillary Clinton's New York senatorial campaign.

Apparently, in the quest to secure the maximum number of votes for Hillary Clinton, the community of New Square became the apple of her campaign's eye. The leadership of New Square was approached and courted by Hillary's campaign, and then the votes were counted on Election Day. In the last election, the town's turnout was a mere 51 percent. However, in November 2000, the figure soared to a staggering 82 percent of registered voters in the Hassidic enclave. Perhaps even more remarkable, out of 1,412 votes cast for senator, Mrs. Clinton obtained all but a handful!

What were the reasons for this purity of electoral support for Hillary Clinton, at a ratio normally encountered in sham elections conducted in third world dictatorships? Perhaps the good citizens of New Square, due to their religious insight, had the ability to comprehend the super-human leadership qualities the aspiring senator claimed for herself, to an extent unmatched by the mere mortals found elsewhere in the State of New York. Or, maybe there is an explanation that has far more to do with the profane then that which is sacred.

In December of 2000, following her successful bid for the Senate, Hillary Rodham Clinton and her husband, President William Jefferson Clinton, met jointly with supporters of the four convicted New Square swindlers, who were serving their sentences in prison.

Though neither Senator Clinton nor Bill Clinton have ever given a cogent explanation of what was discussed (or promised) during this encounter, what followed in the final days and hours of the Clinton administration leaves little to human imagination.

The United States attorney in New York, Mary Jo White, who had prosecuted the New Square swindlers, was informed in the last days of Clinton's presidential administration that the four imprisoned felons were to receive a full presidential commutation, and be released from prison. Though strongly opposed to this wanton display of inexplicable clemency, the late notification insured that her office would be powerless to stop Clinton from proceeding.

Despite her presence at the meeting with the New Square representatives, Hillary Clinton has strenuously denied any knowledge of her husband's intentions to grant presidential pardons to individuals who were strongly supported by her voting constituents from the Hassidic enclave in Rockland County. Yet, anecdotal and direct evidence makes it very clear that, at least on the political level, if not necessarily in their marital relationship, Bill and Hillary Clinton operate as an inseparable team. It stands to reason, therefore, that Bill Clinton's character in relation to his use of political power mirrors that of his wife, and is a window into her own unique ethos.

Bob Herbert, a liberal columnist for The New York Times, wrote on February 26, 2001, that, "You can't lead a nation if you are ashamed of the leadership of your party. The Clintons are a terminally unethical and vulgar couple, and they've betrayed everyone who has ever believed in them."

For a brief interval, liberal Americans were united with their conservative co-citizens in universal outrage at the blatant disregard for even the most basic of ethical norms. After enduring eight years of sleazy fundraising and philandering by their president, it seemed as though all Americans finally got it: Bill Clinton was a man without a moral or ethical compass, and ditto for his wife.

Unfortunately, the intervening years of Bush ineptitude and arrogance have dulled the memories of many Americans, replacing malignant disgust with benign nostalgia. It is this selective memorization of the Clinton presidency-and Hillary's role in that administration-that is an essential preliminary to launching a successful presidential campaign by the former First Lady.

The sordid conclusion of Clinton's presidential regime was merely a dramatic bookend compressing volumes of corruption and sleazy behavior. Bill Clinton was certainly a maverick. In both his political and personal behavior, he displayed an impressive level of skill, not in statecraft, but in outright deception and skullduggery.

Bill Clinton's facility with trashing the truth originates at the dawn of his political career, when he served multiple terms as governor of Arkansas. While he and Hillary were supposedly enjoying a "wonderful" marriage, Governor Clinton was having numerous private encounters with a beautiful woman named Gennifer Flowers.

In 1992, as the Clintons embarked on their first presidential campaign, Ms. Flowers went public with details of what she described as a 12-year covert romantic affair. With the critical New Hampshire primary looming, Bill Clinton resorted to his basic instinct, which was to deny everything.

Unfortunately for the aspiring presidential candidate, Gennifer Flowers had secretly recorded several of their intimate conversations. The recordings were played at a press conference, and received wide media exposure. It appeared that not even Mr. Clinton's ability to offer a forceful and adamant denial would salvage his now crippled presidential bid. However, neither Gennifer Flowers, nor the pundits and political analysts, had reckoned with Bill Clinton's most potent political ally and partner, his wife.

In a frantic though ultimately successful bid to salvage her husband's campaign, as well as her own future ambitions, Hillary Clinton made her first entry into the world of American major media, especially television. While decrying claims that she was merely "standing by her man," she, in effect, stood by her man, and by extension, her ticket into the White House. She displayed a capacity to deny the allegations of philandering by her husband that frankly exceeded that of Bill Clinton's. When confronted with excepts from the Flowers tapes that had her husband refer repeatedly to Ms. Flowers as "Honey," Hillary Clinton was quick to explain to incredulous journalists that this was a common expression in the State of Arkansas, and that nothing untoward could even be remotely inferred from such words.

As history records, Bill Clinton did lose the pivotal New Hampshire primary, but went on to reverse his fortunes, earning the political moniker of "the comeback kid." Among his advisors, it was recognized and acknowledged that Hillary Clinton was a key player on the campaign team, and had fulfilled a crucial role in deflecting and ultimately neutralizing any allegation that could have terminally crippled Bill Clinton's presidential aspirations, as well as her own.

Hillary Clinton played along with the facade that she and her husband had a great marriage, and all the rumors about "Slick Willie's" extra-marital affairs could be dismissed as mere lies, invented by right-wing fanatics. However, after Bill Clinton was reelected for his second term as president, his inability to "keep it in his pants" would derail both his own predilection for demolishing truth with flat denials, and Hillary's impressive skills in providing tactical air support for her husband's blatant lies.

What would become known as "Monicagate" or the Monica Lewinsky scandal, had its origins, in typical Clintonian style, with another woman, a former Arkansas state employee, Paula Corbin Jones. According to Ms. Jones, on May 8, 1991, she was summoned into the hotel room of then Governor Bill Clinton, being escorted by a state trooper, who closed the door after Jones entered the room. Thereupon, alleged Paula Jones, Clinton subjected her to crude sexual advances and harassment. As evidence of what occurred in that hotel room, Paula Jones would claim that Governor Clinton exposed himself in a manner that would enable Ms. Jones to identify "distinguishing characteristics" regarding Bill Clinton's genitals and penis. Three years later, on May 6, 1994, Paula Jones filed a sexual harassment lawsuit against the now President Clinton.

As to be expected, President Clinton denied allegations of sexual misconduct. However, he was now involved in a legal proceeding, and the powers of the presidency, awesome as they are, could not insulate him from legal culpability. It was in this context that lawyer Bill Clinton betrayed his Yale legal training, and walked into a well-laid trap.

The attorneys representing Paula Jones had been supplied with information suggesting that Monica Lewinsky, then a 22-year-old

White House intern, was having an affair with the president. During legal testimony in his sworn deposition, Clinton was subjected to questioning about his alleged extra-marital escapades, to establish a pattern of behavior. Among the questions posed to him was one involving confirmation or denial that he was sexually intimate with Monica Lewinsky. By instinct, Clinton sought safety in his firm denial, and in the process, fell into an ambush which nearly destroyed his presidency, while distracting the American political system for months, ignoring critical developments abroad and at home, including the initial planning by Al-Qaeda that would eventually lead to the 9/11 attacks.

Unknown to the 42nd president, Monica Lewinsky had shared intimate details of her trysts involving Clinton with a friend and co-worker in the Defense Department, Linda Tripp. And, unknown to Ms. Lewinsky, Tripp secretly recorded their spicy conversations. This source material enabled Paula Jones's attorneys to ambush Clinton, whose denial in a legal deposition constituted perjury and obstruction of justice.

In January of 1998, the Internet-based Drudge report dropped the first bombshell regarding Bill Clinton's affair with Monica Lewinsky and the legal predicament it had created in connection with the sexual harassment lawsuit launched by Paula Jones. A week later, the Washington Post had its own bombshell, and a wild media circus was now in full feeding frenzy mode.

On January 26, 1998, Bill Clinton held his first press conference since disclosure of the Lewinsky dalliance. Uncharacteristically for the normally smooth, slick President Clinton, he appeared flustered and awkward, while resorting to his proven practice of trivializing all allegations, and issuing steadfast denials. Protesting that these "false" accusations were undermining his efforts to work on behalf of the American people, and how the unjustified questioning by the media was taking away time he badly needed to work on his forthcoming State of the Union address, he unleashed a rhetorical denial of all wrong-doing which, in its self-righteous intonations, set a new record for cynicism, even for so experienced a practitioner as Bill Clinton:

> "Now, I have to go back to work on my State of the Union speech. And I worked on it until pretty late last night. But I want to say one thing to the American people. I want you to listen to me. I'm going to say this again. I did not have sexual relations with that woman, Miss Lewinsky. I never told anybody to lie, not a single time, never. These allegations are false. And I need to go back to work for the American people."

Though the president appeared unsure of himself, despite the pompous bombast of his impromptu oratory, his most important political ally and confidant was prepared to offer a much smoother and skillful rebuttal for the mass media's consumption. Hillary Clinton was about to make her own foray into the emerging Monica Lewinsky scandal, and in the process, create a Clintonian rationale that would earn its destiny as one of the most pernicious verbal appeals to paranoia as a means of diversion from the real issue at stake. Before elaborating on Hillary Clinton's now-infamous appearance on NBC's *The Today Show*, we should try to comprehend Hillary's motivation for making such a strident public defense of her husband.

The former First Lady has consistently maintained a facade that she has had a "good marriage," with the odd issues that all couples must contend with. In her ghostwritten "autobiography," *Living History*, the conclave of writers working for Hillary Clinton created a script that had her claiming that she believed her husband's denials about sexual relations with "that woman," and was caught totally by surprise when the truth finally was disclosed, shorn of any ambiguity.

Though some may believe this limp explanation, it is probably safe to say that the overwhelming majority of the American people, with their innate common sense, find such a protestation patently absurd. While Mrs. Clinton is derided by many Americans, few will doubt that this shrewd lawyer is a woman of high intelligence and cunning, and therefore, unlikely to be easily fooled. With the well-known pattern of allegations and pending harassment suit concerning allegations of her husband's infidelity, it is hard to imagine that Hillary Clinton was not fully cognizant of the strong possibility that President Clinton was having "sexual relations" with a 22 year old White House intern.

There has been much speculation in the public arena regarding the nature of Bill and Hillary's marriage. Some have suggested that they have an open marriage. Variations on this theme speculate that Hillary Clinton is a lesbian, and accepts that Mr. Clinton requires periodic heterosexual encounters with other women. Whatever the truth may be, it must be recognized that it is highly likely that Hillary Clinton made her appearance on *The Today Show* with intentions, motivations and objectives identical to those her husband displayed at his earlier press conference.

In a never-to-be-forgotten example of televised political soliloquy, the First Lady indignantly protested on behalf of her husband that, "The great story here for anybody willing to find it, write about it and explain it, is this vast right-wing conspiracy that has been conspiring against my husband since the day he announced for president."

"Vast right-wing conspiracy" now became the penultimate defense of Bill Clinton. As a strategy for diversion, it was brilliantly conceived and executed. The liberal Democrats who had been demoralized by the initial allegations were reinvigorated. The media whose bias gravitated towards the Clinton agenda now had the "conspiracy" antidote to the toxic allegations of sleazy sexual escapades and obstruction of justice. The architect of this stratagem, as well as its inseparable spokesperson, was none other than Hillary Rodham Clinton.

It almost worked. The hypocrisy of Clinton's Republican opponents added weight to Hillary's allegation and diatribe, in the minds of many uncertain Americans. However, neither the manipulative brilliance of Hillary Clinton nor the cunning deviousness of Bill Clinton could overcome one severe handicap: the evidence.

As the Monicagate scandal surfaced, Judge Kenneth Starr had been leading the investigation of the Office of the Independent Counsel in the Whitewater affair, regarding allegations of wrongdoing in an Arkansas land transaction involving the Clintons. The Whitewater investigation was moving slowly, and ultimately would not implicate the Clintons in claims of wrongdoing. However, once the Monica Lewinsky matter arose, Judge Starr ran with it. He displayed bulldog tenacity in uncovering evidence that President Clinton had lied under oath. As history was to prove, evidence there was, of the most sordid kind.

To begin with, there were several hours of Linda Tripp's recorded conversations with Lewinsky. Ultimately, under a grant of immunity, Monica Lewinsky testified under oath before a grand jury that she indeed did have a number of sexual encounters in the White House. The grand jury must have been transfixed as Lewinsky responded to legally framed questions about her intimate encounters with Bill Clinton, giving precise details as to their character. As the details became publicly heralded as the leading news by the nation's media,

Americans would require a strong stomach to take in all the sordid details.

According to Ms. Lewinsky, she and the president engaged in oral and anal sex, in various areas of the West Wing of the White House, as well as the Oval Office, which pundits would soon nickname the "Oral Office." Americans learned not only the details of what she did for the president to sexually satisfy him, but also of what he did for her, in particular, with the insertion of a cigar into an orifice of the young White House intern.

The Clintons may have still thought that "Slick Willie" could deny everything, his word against that of a "fantasizing" young woman, who made up everything she relayed to Linda Tripp. Unfortunately, in one of the taped conversations with Ms. Tripp, Lewinsky mentioned that she still retained a blue dress with a semen stain as a souvenir of one of her sexual encounters with Bill Clinton. Linda Tripp very thoughtfully advised her friend not to take the dress to the dry cleaners, then informed Kenneth Starr's investigators that forensic evidence was there for the taking. As history records, they confiscated the dress, and FBI analysis confirmed that the stain on Monica Lewinsky's now iconic blue dress did indeed contain the presidential DNA.

Even William Jefferson Clinton knew the game was up, at least in flatly denying the allegations. On August 17, 1998, Clinton testified before the grand jury that he had an "improper physical relationship" with Lewinsky. He would appear that evening in a nationally televised broadcast, conceding that he had misled the American people about the nature of his liaison with Monica Lewinsky, and that he indeed had an "inappropriate relationship" with the intern.

This time, Hillary Clinton would not appear in a supportive role on television. There would not be a repeat of the diversionary clarion call about a vast right-wing conspiracy. It is hard to believe that she was surprised at the veracity of the allegations. However, we can grant that she was utterly humiliated by the stupidity of her husband, leaving forensic evidence of his extra-marital activity. An utterly reckless act of carelessness by Bill Clinton really did threaten his presidency, and by extension, at some point in the future, her own.

Like vultures circling their prey, the Republican Party, which now controlled both the Senate and House of Representatives, homed in for the kill. Ignoring the preference of the American people, verified by numerous public opinion polls, for a bipartisan motion of censure, which would have been approved overwhelmingly by both Democrats and Republicans, the Republican leadership decided to mount a full-fledged effort at impeachment and dismissal of President Clinton.

What ensued was a demonstration of the amoral opportunism and disingenuous cynicism of both political parties. The Republicans clearly had the votes for impeachment in the House of Representatives. Once impeached, the constitution required that the Senate formally try Clinton for removal from office. Despite their control of the Senate, the Republican Party lacked the two-thirds vote required for Senate conviction. Though Clinton could be impeached, there existed zero mathematical probability that he would be removed from office. All that would be achieved, in the final analysis, was a sleazy diversion from urgent national priorities for months, in the process making America the laughing stock of the world.

By choosing impeachment over censure, the Republicans actually handed Clinton the means of salvaging his presidency. Though Bill Clinton had clearly committed "high crimes and misdemeanors" by his blatant act of perjury, in the minds of most Americans, lying about marital infidelity was not viewed on the same level as the Watergate scandal, which demolished Richard Nixon's presidency. They also miscalculated in believing that they could humiliate Bill Clinton by revealing sordid details concerning his oral sex with Monica Lewinsky. As they would soon learn, the Republican leadership underestimated the narcissism of both Bill Clinton and his wife, and their collective ability to transcend Bill Clinton's sleazy behavior. President Clinton, in particular, would demonstrate an almost superhuman capacity to insulate himself from feelings of shame and humiliation.

As the impeachment process wore on, the Republican leadership would soon have to face some embarrassing revelations of its own.

Congressman Henry Hyde, who chaired the House Judiciary Committee that spearheaded the impeachment effort, had a few skeletons of his own rattling in the closet. As it transpired, he had also carried on an extra-marital affair, and he was by no means the only Republican in that category, passing judgement on Bill Clinton. Their claims that their own covert sexual escapades and wife-cheating were not nearly as bad as Bill Clinton's because the president had carried on his deception while under oath, somehow struck the average American as hypocritical. It would be this hypocrisy which would prove to be Bill Clinton's greatest ally.

Switching gears, the Clinton defenders now embraced Clinton's sexual infidelity, and claimed the Republican attack on the Democrat president was based on sex, and only coincidentally on the act of perjury. Incredibly, in his own testimony before Judge Starr's grand jury, the discredited president maintained he did not lie when he denied having a sexual relationship in his earlier deposition. His defense was remarkable for its intellectual gymnastics, if not candor. According to President Clinton, it all depended on what was meant by the word "is," and besides that, he did not consider oral sex and intimate acts with a cigar to constitute "sexual relations," insofar in how he understood the term.

While the impeachment process was underway, in December 1998, Clinton pulled another rabbit out of his basket of tricks, this time with a "wag the dog" maneuver. Cruise missiles were fired at some tents in Afghanistan and an aspirin factory in Sudan, all allegedly Al-Qaeda installations. What would be dubbed the "Monica Missiles" were viewed by many skeptical Americans as an attempt to divert attention from Clinton's impeachment, and enhance his image as a still-functioning commander-in-chief, unaffected by the Monicagate affair.

On February 12, 1999, the Senate rejected the two articles of impeachment, which had been submitted by the House of Representatives. For more than a year, the Monica Lewinsky scandal had sucked the oxygen out of the American political establishment. A sleazy and disgusting soap opera had been scripted by both political parties, but had been given life by the guttersnipe character of William Jefferson Clinton. In the process, critical threats to America's national security, such as the Iranian and North Korean covert nuclear weapons programs and Al-Qaeda's evolving plot to attack the American homeland, were ignored. Elected officials, senior government officials and mainstream media had preferred to spend more than a year hurling mud at each other, while storm clouds were gathering.

If Bill Clinton had any sense of honor, he would have resigned, and spared America from the national embarrassment of having his dirty laundry literally aired in public and before a global audience, in the process bringing ridicule onto the entire nation. Based on what we now know of President Clinton's character, it would have been surprising if he had made a decision which would have placed his nation's interests above his own. However, it is this author's conviction that a much more potent force than Bill Clinton's own selfishness and narcissism kept him in the desperate fight to save his tarnished presidency. Hillary Clinton's ambition ruled above all else.

Had Bill Clinton resigned the presidency, he would have been permanently viewed by history as a disgraced president. Being the spouse of a discredited president who had been forced to resign in shame, would undoubtedly have been terminally crippling to Hillary's well-laid plans to build a foundation for her own future presidential ambitions. It was essential for Hillary Clinton that her husband fight the impeachment battle, knowing full well that the Republicans lacked the necessary votes in the Senate for conviction.

There is an image that Hillary helped create that the emergence of irrefutable evidence of her husband's infidelity shocked her, and severely affected her marriage, at least for a time. Whatever impact those revelations may have had on their bedtime intimacy, there is substantial indication that Hillary Clinton was a very active participant in crafting and orchestrating her husband's impeachment defense. This time, she abstained from a public role, wisely avoiding an opportuntity to be questioned on her original "vast right-wing conspiracy" theory. However, behind the scenes, the First Lady was a very important player on the team that ultimately achieved a not insignificant measure of success in salvaging the Clinton presidency. A clear indication of their effectiveness can be garnered by the mid-term elections, which actually showed an increase in support for the Democratic Party. To a large extent, Hillary Clinton and her cohorts transformed the impeachment battle into a referendum on the hypocrisy of the Republican Party in having its own wife-cheaters stand in judgement of President Clinton.

Having survived the impeachment battle, it was essential that Hillary's husband enhance his now shoddy image, so that his legacy as president would be a benefit, and not an albatross, to her own eventual presidential bid. This objective was so crucial to Hillary Clinton, it need not matter that innocent lives were sacrificed on the altar of Hillary's political lust and ambitions. Thus began "Operation Allied Force" on March 17, 1999, a bombing campaign against Serbia that endured for weeks, in the process snuffing out the lives of thousands of innocent men, women and children.

The conflict in the former Yugoslavia involved atrocities on all side. The Serbian government had its share of guilt, but so did the other nationalities involved in what was, in effect, the continuation of a centuries old Balkan tribal conflict. The Clinton administration decided to pick one side in this tragic conflict, and engage in massive aerial bombardment of Serbian towns and cities, without a congressional declaration of war or a cogent explanation to the American people of what vital American interests were at stake, warranting such a violent application of military force. As no critical American interests were in fact at stake, the Clintons clearly thought such an attempt at an explanation would be a waste of time.

The carnage inflicted on the Serbian people by the Clinton administration was so wanton and indiscriminate, the U.S. Air Force even bombed the Chinese embassy in Belgrade, the Serbian capital, in the process slaughtering several Chinese diplomats. However, as allegations have surfaced regarding Bill Clinton's acceptance of campaign contributions linked to the Chinese army, it is possible that Beijing will not hold this brutal violation of their Serbian embassy as a permanent grudge.

The "collateral damage" stemming from the Serbian bombing campaign was at least generating media focus on Bill Clinton acting as commander-in-chief, slowly beginning the process of bringing a collective state of amnesia to the American people's consciousness about the Monica Lewinsky scandal. Rebuilding Bill Clinton's reputation as president would enhance Hillary's own long-term career objective. Then, an unanticipated opportunity opened up, placing Hillary Clinton's political ambitions on the fast track. The Clintons had some house hunting to do in the State of New York.

CARPETBAGGER SENATOR

When New York's senior senator, Daniel Patrick Moynihan, announced his decision not to run for re-election in 2000, Hillary Clinton smelled gold. Just as her husband's political career would be ending as his second term as president came to its inevitable end, hers would just be starting. She recognized that for her to return to the White House on her own ticket, she must first build her own political alibi. Serving as senator from the State of New York would be the ideal launching pad for an eventual run for the presidency.

New York had many positive attractions, from Hillary Clinton's perspective. Though it would mean moving to a state in which she had never been domiciled in before, there was probably no more tolerant state in the union towards carpetbagger politicians. She would undoubtedly have been familiar with the precedent established by the late Senator Robert Kennedy, who had relocated to New York, been elected its senator, then began a strong presidential campaign which might have taken him to the White House, had he not been martyred by an assassin's bullets.

Being elected as the junior senator from New York would potentially be an outstanding base upon which to launch a future bid for the presidency. Hillary realized that as a senator from New York, in an eventual effort towards securing the Democratic Party's presidential nomination, she could count on the very large bloc of delegates representing the state to vote for her at the nominating convention. During a presidential election against a Republican opponent, the political history of the last century would have informed her of the near certainty of her receiving the very substantial number of electoral votes from New York State. Senator Moynihan's retirement was indeed a gift from heaven.

Securing the nomination for the New York Democratic Party's nomination as it senatorial candidate for the 2000 election was relatively easy. The Democratic establishment in New York fell into her hands like soft putty. That was the easy part. Far more challenging would be defeating her likely Republican challenger, or so it appeared at the time.

New York City's Republican mayor, Rudy Giuliani, had announced his intention to run for New York senator. Though coping with some negative issues such his marital problems and allegations of police brutality, Giuliani was still perceived as a popular figure among many residents of New York State. He also had the significant advantage of a quantifiable track record in New York as a public servant, including several years as a federal prosecutor with a strong reputation for pursuing organized crime. He had served two terms as mayor of the nation's largest city, and many New Yorkers, including Democrats, credited Giuliani with the city's economic renaissance and reduction in crime. In contrast, Hillary Clinton had no significant record in public service to stand on, either in New York or elsewhere in the country.

Bill and Hillary Clinton bought an expensive home in Chappaqua, an affluent suburban oasis in Westchester County. She could now claim New York residency. More importantly, the aspiring senatorial candidate would soon receive unexpectedly good news for her campaign. Rudy Giuliani, who would have been a formidable opponent, was diagnosed with prostrate cancer. His health problems forced New York City's mayor out of the senate race. In his place, the New York Republican Party nominated Rick Lazio, a congressman from Suffolk County, Long Island. Lazio would prove to be a weak and inept opponent, easily outmaneuvered by Hillary Clinton.

Having been the breadwinner in the Clinton family, standing by her man no matter what, it was time to collect her just reward. Bill Clinton faithfully delivered. Though his reputation was sullied in much of the country, he was still popular in New York, and brought the glamour and prestige of the presidency to Hillary's Senate campaign.

More importantly, there was no more skilled, slick and accomplished political campaigner than Bill Clinton. He was master of front-faced baby kissing and orator of meaningless promises. More importantly, he had mastered the art of backroom fundraising. He knew better than most that money was the mother's milk of America's corrupt politics. A president who would literally rent out rooms at the White House to large political contributors clearly had nothing to learn from other fundraising politicians and consultants. However, there was a great deal that he could teach.

Hillary Clinton benefited from "Slick Willie's" tutoring. She learned the art of campaigning, making meaningless speeches, and raising big money for her campaign. She was not only receiving a crash course in conducting a senatorial campaign. The First Lady was getting an advanced preview of the essential ingredients required in the brutal world of presidential campaigning. However, her own ambition, insatiable ego and innate cunning made her a very quick study, under Bill Clinton's guidance and counseling.

There were times, however, when Hillary's egotistical character and shrillness would bleed through the hired speechwriters' carefully crafted prose, such as when she first announced her intentions to run for the Senate. Her voice became hysterical, jumping several octaves, while her cheekbones protruded with excitement, simultaneously with her eyes glaring with hypnotic intensity.

At the moment when she made official her political intentions, did she become temporarily mesmerized with her own self-importance? Perhaps the First Lady was in a trance, imagining herself returning to the White House as the nation's first woman president. Whatever it was, this outpouring of megalomaniac exuberance disturbed many that observed it. This perception of wide-eyed-egomania would prove a far greater hurdle for Hillary Clinton to overcome than the mediocre campaign conducted by Congressman Lazio.

Despite her perceived and real negatives, Hillary Clinton overcame all obstacles. She made amazing promises to New Yorkers, particularly the residents of economically downtrodden upstate New York. The promises flowed like lava from a resurgent volcano. She would provide 200,000 jobs, tax credits, and other wonderful gifts. Of course, a senator is neither a governor nor a president. She had no ability to affect economic policy in the State of New York as senator. But that was irrelevant. What was important was not such a mundane matter as accuracy and truthfulness. What counted were votes, not scruples. As we have already seen with her campaign's interaction with the uniquely mesmerizing community of New Square, the First Lady and her husband were more than accommodating, if such flexibility translated into votes.

With William Jefferson Clinton to guide her, Hillary had an army of campaign consultants and experts at her call, financed by the tens of millions of dollars she successfully raised from supporters. Between her and Rick Lazio, nearly 80 million dollars would be spent on the 2000 New York senatorial campaign.

On November 7, 2000, Hillary Clinton defeated Lazio with 55% of the votes cast. However, that was not the only good news. With Al Gore's defeat to George W. Bush, which awaited a Supreme Court decision several weeks later, making jest of Gore's triumph in the popular vote, a vacuum had been created within the ranks of the Democratic Party's political establishment. It was not only Gore's defeat, but also Bill Clinton's retirement, which left a deficit of candidates with a national image. Hillary Clinton was prepared to take full advantage of that opportune situation.

With George W. Bush's inauguration as president, First Lady Hillary Clinton now became Senator Hillary Clinton. After decades of supporting her husband's political image, she was about to create her own. However, she received sound advice to start off slow, learn the ropes of the U.S. Senate, and confound the expectations of her critics who expected her to begin as a shrill and noisy debutante.

Among Hillary's vices and virtues, she has an admirable streak of self-discipline, a quality obviously lacking in her husband. Her first months as senator were spent in an uncharacteristically low-key posture. She allowed her senior Democratic colleague from New York, Senator Charles "Chuck" Schumer, to initially grab most of the media spotlight. Senator Clinton familiarized herself with Senate rules and procedures. She built a strong and loyal staff, both in the Senate and with her constituency offices in New York. Most importantly, she obtained Senate committee assignments that were strategically selected to fortify her credentials in areas she was perceived as weak in, in particular, the Armed Services Committee. She was truly thinking ahead to a time when she would be running for the presidency, and would need to create an image as being a strong advocate of national defense.

Hillary Clinton also mounted a charm offensive, building cordial working relationships, especially with her Republican opponents sitting across the aisle. This was all an inseparable component of a public relations offensive aimed as deconstructing the negative image many Americans still had of Hillary as being a shrill, pompous and overly ambitious woman.

For months the junior senator from New York bid her time, softened some of her rough edges, made frequent constituency visits to all parts of New York, and learned the ropes concerning the various committees she sat on. She would wait until the right moment arose before asserting herself. To her surprise, and everyone else's horror, that moment came far sooner than anyone expected.

On September 11, 2001, America was shaken from her myopic complacency. The illusory belief that since the end of the Cold War America was immune from the ravages encountered elsewhere in the world was irretrievably shattered. The iconic World Trade Center Twin Towers were demolished, lower Manhattan was saturated with dust and debris, and thousands of employees who worked in New York City were cruelly slaughtered.

In Washington, the Pentagon lay smoldering, and the Capital building itself had apparently been a target, and might have been destroyed if not for the heroism of the passengers on Flight 93, which was forced down in Pennsylvania before the hijackers could strike their intended target.

The hijacked airliners had killed more Americans than the Japanese armed forces with six aircraft carriers accomplished in their attack on Pearl Harbor. Al-Qaeda's boldly-conceived atrocity had changed the course of history, as well as American politics. The former First Lady was now vaulted to a position of national prominence.

The savvy senator took full advantage of the media opportunities created in the wake of 9/11. She was a highly visible spokesperson for the interests of New York State and New York City, insuring she received full credit for the national outpouring of generosity in providing financial aid to the afflicted region. In the process, her national prominence was enhanced. More and more, her public relations outreach was changing the American public's perception of her. The perception of Hillary as wife of President Clinton, and former First Lady, was quickly receding amongst many segments of the public. To an accelerating degree, she was increasingly being seen as a national political figure in her own right. The opportunity presented by the Al-Qaeda attacks on September 11, 2001 would not be the first instance in which tragic developments would be exploited by Senator Clinton in furthering her political image, however, it is noteworthy and instructive as a precedent which would be repeated.

Seeing years ahead, Hillary Clinton recognized a major vulnerability in any future presidential bid was her lack of credentials and expertise on national defense. Her critics, she realized, would stereotype her as a "liberal," soft and ignorant on questions of national security. However, she had learned from a master on how to put one's hand to the wind, and tack right. Bill Clinton was her role model, and she followed his lead.

In the wake of 9/11, she could position herself from both her roles on the Armed Services Committee and a senator from martyred New York as an apostle on homeland security, a new term in the American political lexicon which would soon become pregnant with transcendent significance.

Hillary Clinton morphed from being the wife of a Vietnam-era draft dodger to a poster child of the clarion call, "We support our troops." She was strongly supportive of the American military intervention in Afghanistan and overthrow of the pro-Al-Qaeda Taliban regime. She visited American forces in Afghanistan in her role as a member of the Armed Services Committee, while her PR people and political staffers insured a plethora of photo ops, print articles and television appearances in the mainstream media. One of the U.S. Army's regular formations, the 10th Mountain Division, is stationed in Fort Drum, New York and has been deployed to Afghanistan. Senator Clinton was strategically photographed, on several occasions, with personnel from the 10th Mountain Division.

The carpetbagger senator representing New York was beginning to create the resume that had been lacking in 2000, when she began her political odyssey. She now had material for future campaigns, state and national. She would lay claim to everything good happening in New York, the large federal funding for New York City made available after 9/11, and being strong on homeland security.

While Hillary was buttressing her image and national profile, her husband was doing his part. After an initial public relations disaster when he chose a posh Manhattan location for his office as a former president, Bill got the message and moved his office uptown, to Harlem. That quieted the critics. Through lucrative speaking engagements and a book contract, he became, for the first time, the breadwinner in the Clinton household. He calibrated his public pronouncements and support of various causes in a manner designed to rehabilitate his image and encourage the public-at-large to forget his ethical and moral lapses. This was all calculated to benefit Hillary.

One crucial strategic decision Hillary probably made early on was to be patient, and forego an early run for the presidency in 2004. As a frontline observer during her husband's two terms at the White House, she understood by instinct how potent the power of presidential incumbency is. Unless George W. Bush was a poor president or lousy campaigner (as was the case with his father, George H. Bush, who was defeated by Bill Clinton when he sought reelection), odds were that he would almost, by default, prevail over his Democratic challenger. The impact of 9/11 and tendency of the American people to rally around their president and commander-in-chief during times of perceived national danger were also undoubtedly factored into the calculation by Hillary and her senior advisors.

Skipping a run in 2004,focussing on her Senate credentials, and running for reelection as New York senator in 2006 would put her in potentially a very strong position to pursue the Democratic nomination for president in 2008. By serving a full six-year term as senator, then running for reelection, Hillary Clinton would largely neutralize the perception of her as a carpetbagger, while acquiring invaluable and successful campaign experience. Making an early decision to sit out the 2004 election was clearly a shrewd political calculation. She also correctly calculated that weak opposition in both the Democratic senatorial primary and November mid-term election assured her of securing reelection with an impressive double-digit margin. Being reelected on those terms would serve her well in a future presidential bid.

Mrs. Clinton was beginning to see her long-held ambition of being American's first female president and commander-in-chief fall into place. The humiliation from the numerous infidelities engaged in by her husband had been a deep personal sacrifice. Probably any other woman in America would long ago have dispensed with such a farcical marital union. However, Hillary was apparently as narcissistic as William Jefferson Clinton was. She could put up with Mr. Clinton's sexual escapades, as long as he delivered on her political objectives. She had been First Lady for 8 years, so embedded into White House decision-making that Mr. Clinton publicly heralded her as a virtual co-president. As President Clinton's image was being rehabilitated, he wrapped his political prestige around his wife, enhancing her own credibility. He infused his long-held political experience in organization, fundraising and campaigning into Hillary, until she became an expert at the art of politicking in her own right.

Hillary Rodham Clinton was following the Clinton lead in pursuing the presidency by focussing solely on image and public perception. She was exhibiting all of Bill Clinton's vaunted skills and expertise as a political grand master and back room dealer. In pure situational analysis and political cunning, she was in some ways even far ahead of her husband, demonstrating a level of subtle cynicism that left more experienced Washington hacks speechless.

Unfortunately for the American people, political cunning and back room stratagems are no substitute for heroic and wise leadership. In the post September 11 world, America was facing unprecedented challenges and dangers, which cried out for mature political judgement and sober leadership.

Hillary Clinton was demonstrating that she could be as clever a politician as was Bill Clinton. Unfortunately, when her first true leadership test arose, Hillary Clinton was to demonstrate that she was as strategically ignorant and cowardly as the very worst of Washington's corrupt political establishment. America was about to go to war, and the senator from New York was in no mood to stop the precipitous advance towards violence.

BETWEEN IRAQ AND A HARD PLACE

In any country, large or small, the most potent powers held by the sovereign, be he or she a king or queen, elected leader or dictator, are those for the making of war. War powers exercised out of a single leader's ego or appetite for foreign conquest have been the scourge of humanity throughout the ages. When war powers have been used justifiably, it has been for the purpose of repelling foreign aggression or preempting a looming and threatening attack.

When the American republic was first conceived, the founding fathers reflected thoughtfully on the many wars waged in Europe by kings and queens lusting for territorial aggrandizement. They were determined to create a strong democratic republic that would have the strength to defend itself, but which would also avoid what America's first president, George Washington, described as "the danger of foreign entanglements." The new democracy would have nothing of the wars of conquest and egotistical pride that had brought misery to much of the planet since the dawn of human civilization.

In their admirable collective wisdom, the founding fathers recognized what the current generation of Americans have long forgotten: the key to America's security and peaceful coexistence with the world is directly rooted in how its war powers are allocated. When the constitution was conceived, it was recognized that no greater danger existed than having the powers to wage war being consolidated into the hands of a single individual.

The first concern the founding fathers had was to protect the nation from a "man on horseback," a military leader who could usurp the nation's civilian leadership and precipitously drag the United States into an unnecessary war. The remedy for this potential danger was to place the armed forces of the United States of America under strict control of the civilian leadership. The way this was accomplished was to place the head of state and government, the president, in the role of commander-in-chief. The president's authority would outweigh that of the most senior general, insuring civilian mastery of the military.

In the process of solving one problem, potentially a more serious danger was created. If the president was commander-in-chief, what prevented him from waking up one morning in a stupor, and deciding to invade another country, without provocation? Clearly, the power to wage war had to be separated from the role of commander of the armed forces. Accordingly, the founding fathers made perhaps their most important finding in arriving at the conclusion that only Congress had the power to declare war. The war powers of the nation would rest in the hands of the peoples' representatives in the legislative branch. If the president as commander-in-chief felt the nation was threatened by attack or had been the victim of aggression, he was duty-bound to appear before Congress and have both houses of the legislative branch approve a formal congressional declaration of war.

Subordinating the powers to wage war to Congress served America well throughout most of its history. When the Japanese navy attacked the United States on December 7, 1941, there could be no doubt that America had just reasons to resort to arms in self-defense. Yet, President Franklin D. Roosevelt understood that he had an absolute obligation, under America's constitution, to appear before Congress and ask for a formal declaration of war against Japan.

The nation had been divided before Pearl Harbor between interventionists and non-interventionists. The requirement for President Roosevelt to consult with Congress and ask for its formal approval of a decision to wage war on Japan brought unity of purpose to the nation. The effectiveness of America's war effort in World War II was directly rooted in the strictly congressional approach exercised by the president in the application of the power to wage war against the enemies of the United States, and mobilize the nation's human and material resources for support of the war effort.

Following World War II and the onset of the Cold War, almost two centuries of congressional oversight of the nation's war powers began to come undone. The Korean War was fought without a formal congressional declaration of war, though President Truman did have congressional support for America's compliance with a United Nation's resolution calling for armed support of the South Korean government to aid it in repelling an attack conducted by North Korea. Technically, the Korean conflict was viewed as a "police action," as opposed to a full-scale war. However, a decade after the Korean War, America intervened in Vietnam in a manner that totally contradicted the carefully laid structures established by America's founding fathers.

If ever there was an unnecessary war, then the penultimate example-before Iraq-was the American war in Vietnam. Ironically, the analysts and consultants, the brightest minds in Washington, who got Vietnam so wrong, were in hindsight far smarter than the neoconservatives, more commonly referred to as neocons, of George W. Bush. There was a Cold War on, communist expansion was feared, leading to the infamous "domino theory," which held that if North Vietnam occupied South Vietnam, all of southeast Asia would turn red, and fall into the laps of Communist China.

We now know that all the calculations were wrong. The leader of North Vietnam and the Viet Cong guerrilla fighters in the south, Ho Chi Minh, was an ardent Vietnamese nationalist. He became a communist, not in the Soviet Union, but in France, where leftist intellectuals convinced him that communism was the most effective framework for liberating his homeland. Ho Chi Minh was also initially pro-American, having lived in Brooklyn for a year. When he prepared the Vietnamese declaration of independence from its French colonial masters, he based it, almost word for word, on the American declaration of independence.

How could America get it so wrong? Almost 60,000 Americans and two million Vietnamese paid with their lives for President Lyndon Johnson's miscalculation. As we now know only too well, Southeast Asia did not fall to the communist hordes. Only a few years after the North Vietnamese defeated the South Vietnamese army, Vietnam and Communist China fought a fierce border war.

When President Johnson's Defense Secretary, Robert McNamara, visited Hanoi several years after the war, he met with the commander of Vietnam's victorious army, the legendary General Vo Nguyen Giap.

"How could such a rich country not have history books?" inquired General Giap. He added that if Americans had read their history before intervening in Vietnam, they would have realized that China and Vietnam had endured one thousand years of mutual hostility. Vietnam could never be a puppet of China's, which was ostensibly the reason for America's military intervention.

The debacle of the Vietnam War cast a long shadow over American society. More than being America's first military defeat, it was the first exposure the American people had to the fallibility of their political leadership. The people of the United States were to painfully learn that their elected representatives and executive leadership had made egregious mistakes and erroneous calculations, while practicing outright lying and deception. History records that the American people were way ahead of the political echelon in concluding that the U.S. had made a fundamental error in intervening in Vietnam to prop up a corrupt military dictatorship, which had been installed by a CIA supported coup. Even the media lagged behind public opinion. Americans understood that they had bet the farm in supporting one side in what was in effect a civil war, which involved no critical national interests of the United States. The fact that the side backed by America lacked the support of the Vietnamese people, and was perceived as puppets serving a new colonial master, became increasingly clear to the American people.

It took a long time for America to recover from the painful ordeal imposed by the Vietnam experience. The people became more skeptical of government, and the American Army had many painful lessons to learn.

A consensus evolved in America at both the political and military level Never again would the United States become involved in a long, protracted guerrilla war or insurgency, in which no vital American interests were at stake. If America did go to war in the future, it would only do so if essential American national security interests were unambiguously at stake. If that were the case, the American military would not strike until it was ready, and would do so with full, overwhelming force. Once the war was victoriously concluded, the armed forces would be withdrawn as soon as practicable. This concept, often referred to as the "Powell Doctrine," named for the former Chairman of the Joint Chiefs of Staff, General Colin Powell, was put into practice in 1991, after the Iraqi army invaded Kuwait. Saddam Hussein's forces were decisively defeated, the Americans wisely avoided the temptation (at that time) of conquering and occupying Iraq, and for more than a decade, the threat of further Iraqi aggression was contained.

The lessons of history seemed to have been learned by the United States, or so it appeared. However, America's corrupt political structures allowed a man to be elected (or appointed by the Supreme Court) as president, who would prove so intellectually vapid, he acted as though the lessons of the Vietnam War were entirely invalid, or perhaps the Vietnam experience had never occurred. George W. Bush, who had assiduously avoided combat during the Vietnam conflict through National Guard involvement that remains controversial, came to the presidency with an apparently irrational obsession with "finishing" his father's job, and being the American conqueror of Baghdad.

Before delving into the Iraq tragedy, it would be instructive to look at the mechanics of how Lyndon Johnson engineered America's massive intervention in Vietnam. He never sought a congressional declaration of war. In truth, it would have been difficult to obtain such a legislative sanction, as North Vietnam never attacked or threatened the territory of the United States. He also wanted to maintain the fiction that America was just providing assistance to a "brave ally," and was not involved in a full-fledged military struggle. As history forces us to recall, Lyndon Johnson had Congress approve the Tonkin Gulf Resolution.

We now know that the Tonkin Gulf Resolution was based on lies. It alleged that the U.S. Navy had been a victim of unprovoked attacks by North Vietnam on two occasions. In fact, the first attack involved American ships violating North Vietnam's territorial waters, in the process of escorting a South Vietnamese commando force that was attempting to attack targets in North Vietnam. There was a lame and ineffectual North Vietnamese response to what was a war-like act by the American ships. The second alleged attack, in fact, never happened.

Based on the most flimsy of pretexts, President Johnson was granted the authorization, under the Tonkin Gulf Resolution, to take whatever actions he deemed necessary as commander-in-chief, to protect U.S. forces. It was that authorization, which eventually sent more than two million American soldiers to Vietnam, incurring all the ghastly consequences referred to earlier. A clear example had been established of the danger of Congress abrogating its war-making powers to the nation's chief executive.

George W. Bush, the nation's 43rd president, lacked the maturity of his father, George H. Bush, who had served as 41st president. Bush, being a bizarre mixture of acute right-wing messianism formed by a simplistic interpretation of evangelical Christianity, combined with a staggering level of intellectual laziness and sheer incompetence, appeared to be an accidental president. How could such a figure rise to serve as America's chief executive? We will have more to say about this in a later chapter.

A man ignorant of history and unwilling to learn from the past will, as the great Spanish philosopher George Santayana so presciently warned, be condemned to repeat the errors of the past. In looking back at the roots which led to America's catastrophic Iraq project, it is as though the Vietnam War never occurred, so compelling would be the repetition of miscalculations, ignorance and outright lies. Sixty thousand dead Americans, there names enshrined forever on the memorial wall along the Potomac, are turning in their graves, grieving at the one tangible benefit of their ultimate sacrifice, the learning of historically urgent lessons, being so frivolously discarded by the worst political leadership in U.S. history. That leadership not only comprised President Bush and his neocon clique of incompetents. They were massively aided and abetted by a Congress that surrendered its historic responsibilities, preferring historical myopia to courage and leadership. Foremost among them would be the junior senator from New York, Hillary Rodham Clinton.

In classic replication of Lyndon Johnson's now infamous Tonkin Gulf Resolution, the war-crazed president submitted House Joint Resolution 114 and Senate Joint Resolution 45, the so-called "Authorization for Use of Military Force Against Iraq Resolution of 2002." As with its Vietnam-era precursor, it was a blank check for waging war. Based on the deceit that Iraq possessed weapons of mass destruction, it granted President Bush the carte blanche right to wage war, unrestricted in its application, if he decided, entirely on his own, that Iraq had not "disarmed" itself of WMDs (which we now know never existed). Every congressman and senator who voted for HJR 114 and SJR 45 knew exactly what they were doing, at least in the short-run. They were voting for violent war, an unprovoked attack against a country that had not attacked the United States. What apparently they were ignorant of were the consequences of their decision, and the historical example of Vietnam, which should have informed them. Hillary Clinton stands among those who are complicit in empowering an inept, stupid man to engineer such a calamitous policy decision, with frightful implications that will haunt America for generations.

When the votes for HJR 114 and SJR 45 were tabulated, there were men and women of courage who did vote against this rush to war. Most were Democrats, but some were Republicans. On October 10, 2002, the House of Representatives voted 296 yea, 133 nay. In the Senate, 77 senators endorsed Bush's lust for war. Twenty-three senators had the moral courage to vote their conscience and common sense, and register their opposition to an unfolding American disaster. Of those senators, 22 were Democrats. They included Senators Edward Kennedy, Russ Feingold and Barbara Boxer. But not Hillary Rodham Clinton.

Contrast Hillary Clinton's vote with that of the lone Republican senator to vote against the authorization for war, Lincoln Chaffee of Rhode Island. Hillary's vote was easy; Chaffee had the tough decision to make in opposing the president, who was from his own political party. As the lone Senate Republican registering opposition to his president's lust for war, he faced disapproval and disdain from his party colleagues. He set an example of what political courage entails. A model of political behavior not to be emulated by Senator Clinton.

Another comparison harks back to the Vietnam era. It involved another "carpetbagger" senator from New York, the late Robert Kennedy, who also harbored presidential ambitions. He was made of sterner stuff than Mrs. Clinton. When it became clear to him that the Vietnam War was a tragic and costly mistake, he courageously broke with President Johnson, and based his presidential campaign on a promise to end the war.

In her Senate speech justifying her decision to surrender Congress's war-making prerogatives to an ignorant adventurer, Hillary Clinton demonstrated the same ability as her husband to meander and obfuscate, tacking in every conceivable direction. She expressed her concern for the risks of engaging in unilateral action, yet she also strangely rationalized why this would be justified. There was something in her speech for partisans who were either for or against the war. Amidst the self-contradicting verbiage scripted by her speechwriters, Senator Clinton said, "I have concluded, after careful and serious consideration, that a vote for the resolution best serves the security of our nation."

The logic was sparse, at least as a rationalization for engaging in war. However, it was not without merit, at least from the standpoint of political expediency. Senator Clinton was clearly weighing her vote in political terms. She wanted to be seen as supporting what public opinion polls at the time suggested was the preference of the American people. However, as with polls conducted in the early stages of the Vietnam War, the American people initially believed their leaders who claimed that the nation was in grave peril from a hostile foreign power.

Hillary's closing words in support of her vote included a phrase that would box her into a corner as the Iraq tragedy unfolded in its full macabre dimensions: "So it is with conviction that I support this resolution as being in the best interests of our nation."

The junior senator from New York had now gone on record as having submitted the most crucial decision a nation can debate, the matter of waging war or peace, to her vaunted leadership skills, and had determined that her conclusion served America's best interests. In her own mind, she could never admit that her vote rendered on October 10, 2002 was a colossal blunder, for to do so, she would be undermining her presidential ambitions.

Four years after the initiation of the awkwardly named "Operation Iraqi Freedom," with 3,000 dead American soldiers, tens of thousands more Americans maimed and more than one hundred thousand dead Iraqi civilians, Bush's Iraq project had all the appearances of unmitigated disaster. Despite President Bush's quick proclamation aboard an aircraft carrier of "mission accomplished" and Vice President Dick Cheney's boastful taunt nearly three years later that the Iraqi insurgency was in its "last throes," the horror was only beginning. America's over-stretched military forces were trapped in a violent insurgency that had evolved into a sectarian conflict that had all the characteristics of a civil war.

It did not take long to discover that WMDs did not exist in Iraq. Before the onset of war, Saddam Hussein had bowed to international pressure, and allowed the United Nations weapons inspectors to survey his country. Despite positive feedback from the UN inspectors, indicating that they were receiving full cooperation from the Iraqi authorities, and had thus far determined that weapons of mass destruction were not present, George W. Bush, empowered by a compliant Congress to wage war on his own whim, decided that the Iraqi cooperation was not acceptable. Accordingly, he unleashed an unprovoked attack on Iraq. It was the abdication of their responsibilities by politicians such as Senator Clinton that enabled Bush to initiate such folly.

Apparently, Bush was foolish enough to believe his equally discordant advisors, including Dick Cheney, secretary of defense Donald Rumsfeld and their neocon clique that taking Iraq would be a cakewalk. Following the submission of Iraq, imagined the hallucinating neocons, amid flower-throwing Iraqi citizens grateful for their supposed liberation, Iraq would become a pro-American bastion in the Middle East, spreading American style governance and economics in the heart of the Moslem and Arab world. It was a reverse of the domino theory that rationalized American intervention during the Vietnam era, and if anything, was even more illogically conceived.

In the months before the long-planned invasion of Iraq, President Bush met with pro-American Iraqis of the type that provided false "intelligence" of Saddam Hussein's alleged mobile biological warfare laboratories and other concoctions. When informed by the group of Iraq's demographic breakdown with respect to Shiites and Sunnis, Bush's response was, "I thought they were all Moslems." That a man of such appalling ignorance could wage war on the flimsiest pretext in so cavalier a manner is the clearest illustration of the dangers of Congress surrendering its war-making powers to the president.

America's invasion of Iraq in 2003 was anchored in neocon delusions. Born of the ambition of a reckless and ignorant man, under the influence of a narrow minded clique of bloodthirsty noncombatants, and propelled by outright deception of the American people, the enterprise was doomed to failure. Beyond the price in precious human lives, the Iraqi adventure has already cost the American people more than 300 billion dollars, at a time of mounting budget deficits and funding cuts in critical human needs areas. Yet, the financial costs may ultimately exceed the worst nightmares of most economists.

Columbia University economist Joseph E. Stiglitz, who won the Nobel Prize in economics in 2001, and Harvard lecturer Linda Bilmes, collaborated on a report that concluded that the total costs of the Iraq war will exceed the staggering and unimaginable figure of *two trillion dollars*! This forecast is based on the gradual drawing down of American forces in Iraq so that they are entirely withdrawn by 2010.

However, many politicians, both Democrats and Republicans, have publicly proclaimed that American forces may need to be stationed in Iraq for the next several decades. Whatever unfolds in Iraq, it is quite clear that many future generations of Americans will be paying for the mad adventure initiated by George W. Bush, and facilitated by irresponsible congressmen and senators, including Hillary Rodham Clinton.

With the butcher's and banker's bills fast accumulating, along with the continual deterioration of Iraq as it slides into irreversible anarchy and violence, the American people have already rendered their verdict. After three years of the Iraq folly, public opinion polls have consistently registered that at least 60 percent of the American people are convinced that the war was a colossal blunder.

Knowing how the American people viewed the war in Iraq, what about the junior senator from New York? Having staked her claim on rendering her support for Bush's war after "careful and serious" consideration, she could not admit that she had made a mistake, unlike some of her colleagues on Capital Hill who did publicly confess their regret for supporting the Iraq War Resolution. On such a critical vote, she must maintain a Clintonian facade of infallibility.

As the body bags piled up and public support for the war plummeted, Senator Clinton embarked upon a strategy that enabled her to avoid admitting that her "careful consideration" had been disastrously flawed. Like all egotistical persons in authority, she pointed the blame elsewhere.

A year after the onset of "Operation Iraqi Freedom," Hillary Clinton appeared on CNN's "Larry King Live." Despite the clear evidence already available, demonstrating that the war had been launched on a basis of lies and was attracting jihadists from all over the world to wage war on the American troops, she self-righteously pontificated to Larry King, "No, I don't regret giving the president authority because at the time it was in the context of weapons of mass destruction, grave threats to the United States, and clearly, Saddam Hussein had been a real problem for the international community for more than a decade."

In continuing to justify the basis for Bush's war and her support of his blank check to initiate hostilities, Senator Clinton was also covering her husband's flank. Bill Clinton had periodically bombed Iraqi targets to demonstrate his prowess as commander-in-chief. The former president had also endorsed the pre-war religion that WMDs in Iraq existed, without a shadow of a doubt. There can be no question of Hillary Clinton dissenting from the perspective of her husband. She had, after all, been his "co-president" during eight years occupancy of the White House.

As president, Bill Clinton gutted the CIA's human intelligence capabilities. Overly reliant on electronic means and unreliable Iraqi "defectors," the Clinton presidency helped build the fraudulent Iraqi intelligence dossier that was cynically exploited by the Bush administration to justify for the American people and the world at large a war they wished to wage for reasons unrelated to WMDs. Hillary Clinton could not afford to contradict the cover story put out by the administration, for to do so would be to undermine the image of her husband's presidency, casting aspersions on her own future presidential bid.

Rather than expressing regret for her decision, she decided to stand by the irrefutable correctness of her vote, and then blame the Bush administration for running a lousy war.

"How could they have been so poorly prepared for the aftermath of the toppling of Saddam Hussein?" Hillary protested to Larry King. Thus was created Hillary Clinton's alibi for her infamous "carefully considered" vote for empowering Bush to wage unprovoked war, without obtaining a congressional declaration of war. Her vote was "correct;" the problem was that George W. Bush, Dick Cheney, Donald Rumsfeld et al were all hopelessly inept in planning and executing a war. The inference war clear: if Senator Hillary Clinton had been the commander-in-chief, all would have been well on the battlefield.

As a growing number of Americans turned thumbs down on the war, many Democrats and even some Republicans who had initially backed President Bush's Iraq adventure turned against it. Potential nominees for the 2008 Democratic presidential nomination who had voted for the Iraq war resolution, including Senator John Kerry (the Democrat 2004 presidential candidate) publicly stated that their votes were a mistake. Voices in Congress labeling the war a disaster, and calling for a timetable for withdrawal of all American occupation troops, have grown louder.

What about New York's junior senator? She had her own game-plan.

Following in the traditions of her husband, she held her hand to the wind, tacking left and right, while avoiding any admission that her vote in support of the war a mistake.

She staked out her position against potential Republican opponents, as well as Democratic contenders for the 2008 presidential nomination.

The Republicans were all incompetents, with no idea how to run a decent war, as no doubt a future President Hillary Clinton would. As for her Democratic challengers who called for withdrawal, that in her view was flat-out wrong. To the contrary, more troops should be sent to Iraq, and as president she would deploy those augmented forces, unlike George W. Bush.

In calling for additional American soldiers to be sent to Iraq, Mrs. Clinton displayed her appalling and dangerous ignorance of military and strategic affairs, in the process whitewashing the disastrous military decisions made during her husband's presidency.

When America first went to war against Iraq in 1991, after Saddam Hussein occupied Kuwait, the United States Army could deploy 16 combat divisions in the field, not including reserve forces. It was this force level that enabled the first President Bush to apply the Powell doctrine, and strike with full and overwhelming force.

Bill Clinton came to the presidency with practically no expertise in military affairs. Though national security is the number one priority for any American president, William Jefferson Clinton brought no intrinsic knowledge of his own to this critical field of responsibility. On the other hand, he harbored disdain for the military, reflected in his contemporary rationalizations for evading military service during the Vietnam War. This cognitive dissonance on the part of Bill Clinton would result in eight years of diminution of America's ability to deploy an army in the field.

Operating under the false premise that the end of the Cold War meant that much of the American Army could be dismantled, President Clinton oversaw the wholesale elimination of entire mechanized formations of the United States Army. By the time he left office, what was once an army of 16 divisions had been reduced to only ten. There were further reductions in the strength of the Army Reserve and National Guard, and a dangerous reduction in battlefield readiness. By the time William Jefferson Clinton left office, it was an impossibility for the United States military to replicate "Desert Storm," the operation that drove Saddam Hussein's forces out of Kuwait in 1991.

When George W. Bush went to war against Iraq in 2003, he did so with Bill Clinton's army. Despite his campaign rhetoric denouncing Clinton's defense policies, there had been no fundamental changes to the table of organization and equipment of the U.S. Army during the period from Bush's inauguration to the onset of "Operation Iraqi Freedom."

As strange as it may seem in retrospect, Bush, Cheney and Rumsfeld were not the least concerned about the impossibility of matching the American military deployment against Iraq in 1991. In their delusional fantasies, they even thought that a force of a few thousand paratroopers could descend on Baghdad, and quickly dispose of Saddam Hussein. They clearly did not seriously prepare for a military occupation of Iraq. If they had given such thought, then they would have realized that America lacked the military means to pursue their ambitions in Iraq. However, they were not alone in their "Alice in Wonderland" journey towards war. They were joined by cheerful hordes from Congress, including Senator Hillary Clinton.

Neither the Bush administration nor Congress can claim that they had no idea of the challenges and difficulties that lay ahead. To the disdain of Donald Rumsfeld, the Army's chief of staff, General Eric Shinseki, gave a truthful and prophetic warning when he testified before the Senate Armed Services Committee, only weeks before the onset of hostilities in Iraq.

The record of General Shinseki's prescient testimony shows no questioning of any noteworthiness by Senator Hillary Clinton. Though aspiring to be president, and one who would later criticize George W. Bush for not raising questions and challenging assumptions in the onrush to war, her own record shows that she was in lock-step with Bush's lack of intellectual curiosity in the mad rush to conquest in the Persian Gulf. It would fall to her Democratic committee colleague from Michigan, Senator Carl Levin, to ask the most pertinent question during that hearing in February 2003, which was how many troops General Shinseki estimated would be required for the occupation of Iraq, once Saddam's army had been defeated.

The Army's chief of staff was a consummate military professional, with a long and distinguished record of service to his country. In reply to Levin's question, Shinseki said, "I would say that what's been mobilized to this point, something on the order of several hundred thousand soldiers are probably, you know, a figure that would be required. We're talking about post-hostilities control over a piece of geography that's fairly significant, with the kinds of ethnic tensions that could lead to other problems. And so it takes a significant ground- force presence to maintain a safe and secure environment, to ensure that people are fed, that water is distributed, all the normal responsibilities that go along with administering a situation like this."

Both defense secretary Rumsfeld and his deputy, Paul Wolfowitz, denounced General Shinseki's carefully considered estimate of the requirements of post-occupation force levels as "wildly off the mark."

We now know that no clairvoyant could have matched the accuracy of Shinseki's prophetic testimony before the Armed Services Committee. And herein lies the ultimate irrationality of the Iraq war, and all those who supported it.

When the French army fought a counter-insurgency war against Algerian rebels in the 1950's, they required an occupation army of 500,000 men. There are many similarities between the insurgency in Iraq and the Algerian conflict of 1954-62, so that the size of the French occupation army in Algeria can be considered a benchmark for what conceivably would be needed for Iraq.

Bill Clinton's army, which President Bush inherited, at full strength, numbered about 450,000 soldiers. This force was required for numerous deployments overseas, training and rotation at home, and preparation for contingencies. Even augmented with reserve forces and the Marine Corps, it is far beyond the capacity of the American armed forces, as currently structured, to maintain a sufficiently large occupation army in Iraq.

Understanding the truth about America's military potential after eight years of Hillary Clinton's husband serving as commander-in-chief, it is simply disingenuous to accept the criticism of individuals such as Senator Clinton that the decision to go to war is beyond reproach, but the Bush administration did not deploy enough troops, for which it should accept sole blame. Mathematically, there were simply no "extra troops" to deploy in Iraq.

Currently, there are approximately 140,000 American soldiers serving with the occupation army in Iraq. As dangerously insufficient as this force is, even this far smaller number than required is beyond the ability of the American military to sustain. Active duty soldiers from the Army and Marine Corps have had to serve three or four tours of duty, breaking their morale and destroying families. Morale has plummeted, resulting in reduced enlistment, which can only be reversed by the Pentagon reducing the standards used for recruitment. The result is a weaker army. Furthermore, even with multiple tours of duty, the army still lacks the manpower for even a significantly deficient army of occupations. National Guard and reserve units are being forced to endure long deployments in Iraq, for a role they were never designed for. When Hurricane Katrina ravaged New Orleans in 2005, badly needed Louisiana National Guard units were stuck in Iraq.

The American people should reflect on a sobering fact. The last time America deployed an army in the field of half a million men was during the VietnamWar. To sustain that army, and meet America's other national security interests and global commitments, required a military draft. To provide the forces General Shinseki warned would be required for a military expedition and occupation in Iraq would have meant that the United States would have had to undergo full mobilization, including restoration of the draft of young men for compulsory military service. It was acute irrationality to believe that an all-volunteer army structured for peacetime, with periodic low-intensity conflicts, could fulfill the neocon and congressional fantasies and illusions in the Middle East. The fact that Congress did not raise these critical issues demonstrates that they share culpability with the Bush administration for the hideous calamity that is the mad Iraq project of the neocon elite.

As an aspiring president and commander-in-chief, Hillary Clinton has much to answer for, in terms of her AWOL performance as a senator during the crucial deliberations that enabled George Bush to precipitate America's catastrophic involvement in Iraq. However, the evidence thus far is that Hillary Clinton will not answer for anything. She will evade, meander and vacillate, blaming others while maintaining the correctness and rectitude of her vote for war.

To buttress her reputation for military "expertise" and "strategic thinking," Senator Clinton participated in a tour of Iraq in February

2005. By then, nearly two years after the invasion of Iraq, a bloody insurgency was well underway. The claim of WMDs in Iraq had been proven to be a sham. No-bid contracts had flushed companies with close ties to the Bush administration with vast sums of money, while the supposed reconstruction of Iraq was proceeding at a snail's pace, at best. In spite of all the evidence to the contrary, Clinton used her trip to Iraq as a platform to echo some of the worst rationalizations of the neocons in Bush's leadership circles.

When asked by a reporter during her Iraq trip for her assessment of the Bush administration's Iraqi project, she replied that she was "cautiously optimistic." Elaborating on her response, she said, "cautious because there are so many challenges, cautious because there are neighbors of Iraq that are not necessarily enthusiastic about the success of the Iraqi people in creating and sustaining a multi-ethnic, multi-religious democracy,"

In a manner worthy of her husband, Hillary Clinton gave a response that covered all potential political contingencies, yet was supportive of the Bush rationale that it was justifiable fighting a war in Iraq for "Iraqi democracy," even if the original justification, WMDs, had proven to be a mirage.

In the summer of 2006, Hillary Clinton's fellow pro-war Democratic senator, Joseph Lieberman, was defeated in the Connecticut primary by his challenger, anti-war candidate Ned Lamont. Prior to his defeat, Clinton openly campaigned for Lieberman, concerned that his defeat would mean the ascendancy of anti-war candidates in the Democratic Party. Such a development could jeopardize her planned presidential campaign, if she maintained the correctness of her pro-war vote.

As the opinion polls tilted towards a likely Ned Lamont victory, Hillary began to engineer some subtle shifts. While continuing to support Lieberman, she stated publicly that if he were defeated and then ran in the general election as an independent candidate, she would support and campaign for the Democrat nominee. In the wake of Lieberman's defeat, she took more drastic action.

As recorded above, Hillary Clinton made an unremarkable impression when General Shinseki appeared before the Senate Armed Services Committee. However, in August 2006, when Donald Rumsfeld testified before the same committee, the former First Lady had much more at stake. While still not conceding the error of her vote for war, she needed to drastically distance herself from the growing public perception of the disastrous war management of the Bush administration. After reading before the television cameras a diatribe concocted by her staffers, saturated with cliches and critiques authored by many others before her, she called for Rumsfeld's resignation.

Literally dozens of other politicians, and even several retired generals, had already publicly called for Rumsfeld to resign, or be fired by the president. In the wake of the Abu Ghraib scandal concerning the mistreatment of Iraqi prisoners by American soldiers, Bill Clinton's vice president, Al Gore, in an emotional speech, demanded that Rumsfeld immediately resign.

There was nothing emotional about Hillary Clinton's rhetorical performance and call for Rumsfeld's elimination. Yet, she had to act as though she was the first political leader on record calling for the dismissal of the secretary of defense. Out of sheer political necessity, she will criticize others for the war's bumbling. What is off the agenda is self-criticism.

As a partner with the 42nd president, who eroded America's military capacity and diminished the quality of human intelligence available to policy makers, Mrs. Clinton must bear significant responsibility for the Iraq debacle. More importantly, as with few other senators and congressmen, she had insight into how fragile and contrived pre-war intelligence was on Iraq and its alleged WMD programs. The culmination of all her previous political involvement was to render a vote with ghastly human consequences, for purely cynical reasons.

History will not be kind to those who engineered the Iraq calamity that will haunt America for decades. George W. Bush and his neocon cohorts will deservedly receive much of the blame. However, history will also record that political opportunists such as Hillary Rodham Clinton engaged in gross dereliction of duty by failing to uphold the sole right of Congress to decide on war and peace. Whatever the future may hold for her, she has already given ample evidence of her unsuitability to serve as America's commander-in-chief.

CELEBRITY POLITICS, IMAGERY AND DYNASTIC RULE

Washington has increasingly taken on the airs of a Babylon on the Potomac. Foreign visitors to the United States are often confused and mesmerized by the superficiality and bizarre showmanship that has come to characterize American politics. Indeed, to fully understand the state of American political culture, one would be well advised to turn towards Hollywood for comprehension and understanding.

To any aspiring actor or actress, receiving Hollywood's Academy Award or Oscar is the "Holy Grail" of their profession. This, despite the fact that serious film critics have long ago written off much of the Academy's award criteria as having little to do with pure creative talent. Serious students of the cinematic arts may know that an Academy Award is more often then not governed by a process more dependent on the effectiveness of a nominee's public relations agent than raw talent. However, this is a fact largely unknown to the public at large.

Winning one Academy Award will raise an actor's career from the bowels of obscurity. Winning a second Oscar may mean a lifetime career of acting contracts at seven and even eight figure payment for each film. Clearly, to an ambitious actor or actress, there is a great deal at stake in connection with Hollywood's annual Academy Awards presentation.

In 2005, a nominee for the category of "Best Actress" was Hilary Swank for her role in "Million Dollar Baby." Having previously won an Academy Award in the same category for "Boys Don't Cry," it would obviously be a great thing if she won a second such award.

No doubt, Ms. Swank is a talented actress. However, so presumably were all the other contenders that year for Hollywood's judgement on "Best Actress." Fortunately for Hilary Swank, she had useful help, which had nothing to do with her acting ability. That help was her public relations. From a PR perspective, it should be clear how useful a positive story on CBS's *Sixty Minutes* would be, especially if broadcast only a few weeks before the Academy made its awards decision.

Having secured a *Sixty Minutes* story by Mike Wallace, Hilary Swank's PR assets undoubtedly understood that what CBS could do for those deliberating on the Academy's jury would be to distinguish their client from the other contenders, not only as a better actress, but also as a better human being. With the stereotype well-embedded in public consciousness that Hollywood personalities have bad marriages and frequent divorces, what better way to highlight Ms. Swank as different from the other "Best Actress" nominees than as a happily married woman, faithfully devoted to her husband?

Mike Wallace, in his narrative of the *Sixty Minutes* pre-Oscar deliberations profile of Hilary Swank, said the following:

> "Today, she and her husband, Emmy-winning actor and inspiring director Chad Lowe, live a quiet life in Manhattan, sharing their town house with a menagerie of animals. The fact is Hilary Swank is about as unpretentious as you can get. She doesn't drink, she doesn't smoke, she's polite, does volunteer work in her community and has been with the same man for 12 years...Swank says she's still deeply in love with her husband and planning for a family, but doing her best to keep her private life private."

A portrait of a very nice woman, with an enduring marriage, was artfully presented to the American people, as well as the Academy Awards jury. As history records, Ms. Swank won her second Oscar, and about a year later, separated from her husband, and shortly afterwards, filed for divorce.

The Hilary Swank example is quite comprehensible within a Hollywood context. After all, actors and actresses get paid to play the roles of other characters and present fantasy as reality. That those skills and dynamics should also be deployed for building an image, not necessarily rooted entirely in reality, to advance an entertainer's career interests should not surprise us.

An over-arching explanation for America's tragic descent into political morass and squalor is that the behavior, methodologies and contrived imagery of Hollywood have infused American politics to a level that is clinically toxic. By understanding the example of Hilary Swank's *Sixty Minutes* profile and the construction of a celebrity image, we in the process enhance our comprehension of how American politics now functions. Image trumps reality.

For much of American history, a politician's character mattered greatly. Before television and radio conglomerates, public relations spin-meisters, political consultants and speechwriters, there existed the whistle-stop tour, in which a presidential candidate spoke directly to the people. Chances were, if he read a speech, it was one that at least was written by the candidate himself. Imagine if during the Gettysburg Address, Abraham Lincoln had discarded his own brilliant and courageous eloquence, and read something written by one of George W. Bush's speechwriters.

Perhaps the election of Ronald Reagan as America's 40th marked a seminal turning point in American presidential politics. Ronald Reagan *was* an actor, having appeared in dozens of films and television dramas. He even served as president of the Screen Actors, Guild, then successfully transitioned into politics, first as governor of California, and from 1981 through 1989 as a two-term president. His presidential campaigns and tenure were strongly focussed on imagery, a role that a trained actor, well adapted to reading scripts, was admirably suited for.

In the period since the Reagan presidency, American politics have descended to the level of expensive carnivals, overflowing with televised seltzer water, popcorn and beer in lieu of substantive discussion and exploration of issues, political platform and a candidate's character. It is in this degraded political culture that candidates as marginal and severely flawed as Bill Clinton and George W. Bush can become the nation's president and commander-in-chief. For those same reasons, Hillary Clinton can actually become a frontrunner candidate for her party's presidential nomination. Perhaps the old adage is true, that those whom the Gods would destroy, they first render mad.

The inanity and crassness of American politics has persuaded a large segment of the American people to opt out of the process altogether. Barely more than half of all eligible voters actually cast a ballot in an American presidential election. In state, county and local elections the turnout is far lower. Of all the supposed democratic nations on earth, the United States ranks near the bottom in terms of participatory democracy and voter turnout. On the other hand, it ranks at the very top in the amount of money invested by candidates in each vote actually cast. The vast expenditures by political candidates in the United States are devoted towards two priorities; creating an enticing image for the candidate, while demolishing that of his opponent. At the presidential level, this dynamic becomes exponentially magnified.

Imagery has become the center-of-gravity of American presidential politics. Find a candidate that looks attractive to a defined demographic in key states with the appropriate number of electoral votes (the national popular vote be damned), hire speechwriters to come up with clever sound-bites and then convince the American people that those words are actually the authentic product of the candidate's superior intellect. Next, focus on presenting the candidate's opponent as the embodiment of all that is evil. That, in essence, is the "work-plan" of a contemporary American presidential campaign.

Bill Clinton, when running against George H. Bush, was able to defeat an incumbent president, despite his deep character flaws and lack of national experience appropriate to the role of world leader and American commander-in-chief. As a master politician, he made use of his capable and creative staff's rhetorical product, "It's the economy, stupid," and ran circles around his opponent with it. The power of the contrived image of William Jefferson Clinton overcame not only an incumbent president, but also his own weaknesses and personal defects, including the Gennifer Flowers scandal.

The Republicans tried desperately to destroy the Clinton presidency. They hoped that their failed impeachment drive would at least inflict mortal collateral damage on Al Gore's presidential campaign. However, they realized that negative campaigning alone would not guarantee that they would retake the White House. What was required was a candidate with name recognition, around which an image could be constructed. The son of President Bush, George W. Bush, was about to collect his inheritance.

If George W. Bush were not the son of President George H. Bush, would he have been elected president? Would he even have been a contender for that office? To any objective observer, it is extremely doubtful that a man of Bush's mediocrity could even have been a credible candidate.

The same question can be legitimately directed towards Hillary Rodham Clinton. If she were not the spouse of President Bill Clinton and a former First Lady, would she, on her own merit, be as credible and visible a presidential hopeful as she clearly is, at least in the eyes of the American media and political establishment? Not only is it clear that this could never be the case; if she were not the First Lady in 2000, there never would have been a Hillary Clinton senatorial campaign in New York.

Having direct family connections to a former president is perhaps the most potent form of networking and celebrity visibility available to any aspiring politician. This translates in two forms: media attention and ability to raise large sums of money, so critical to political success in the United States of America.

Periodically glance at the newspaper tabloids strategically displayed at the checkout counters of any supermarket in America, and one scans the headlines regarding some innocuous tidbit or extra-marital complication of a celebrity personality. The media have conditioned a large segment of the American population to be obsessed with the lives and perceived image of celebrities. It is within this context that presidential elections in the U.S. have now seen the emergence of the celebrity candidate.

Hillary Clinton is a perceived frontrunner and exceptionally viable candidate due to her celebrity status. Wife of Bill Clinton, former First Lady, these are all considered priceless items of equity within the political marketplace. The reason is simple enough: name recognition.

In the 2008 presidential election, voters will render their judgment on the basis of thirty- second paid television and radio spots, and print media coverage. Hillary's power as a celebrity enables her to be a center of media attention, with high name recognition. She will attract votes far more often due to her status and visibility as a celebrity than she ever could do on the strength of her ideas and "vision" alone.

As with many products of fame, the substance is a long way from perception. That is the whole point of building a candidate's image and celebrity status. A mythology will be created about Hillary Rodham Clinton, attributing amazing qualities of leadership, courage, strategic and economic brilliance, with a heavy does of military expertise thrown in for good measure. Sound bites, clever phrases concocted by speechwriters, endorsement by other celebrities and undoubtedly skillful use of her celebrity husband will substitute for thoughtful dissertation.

In ancient Rome, when the republic was replaced by dynastic imperial rule, emperors had statues of themselves erected, conveying a perception that they were God-like figures of nobility, courage and visionary leadership qualities. In 21st century America, advertising on television, the Internet and print media is the political statuary of contemporary times. However, their role is exactly the same as was the case with Roman imperial statues.

As detailed by historians, more often than not the Roman emperors were men of debauchery, avarice and lustful greed. In other words, totally in contradiction to the image projected by the hands of skilled political masons.

The public relations and political consultants, much as their statue-building predecessors of Imperial Rome, will seek to hide the defects of their candidates, while constructing an exaggerated or false image of their supposed meritorious qualities.

Bill Clinton is a rare example; a politician with a warehouse full of vices, who had virtual statues erected while running for president and reelection and then *after* he had served his term. It is critical to the success of a Hillary Clinton presidential run that her husband not only keep his zipper up; he must campaign again, for the role of ex-president, inducing the American public to enter a state of amnesia, and forget the disgrace that characterized the Clinton presidency. Mr. Clinton must be seen as a selfless public servant, devoting his post-presidential days to fighting AIDS in Africa, raising money for tsunami relief, and simultaneously creating an image that he was a far better president than the disaster-prone George W. Bush. Sublimely, if the American people can be lulled into passively accepting a revisionist view of Bill Clinton's presidency, this will arouse feelings of nostalgia, and a belief that Hillary Clinton can restore the "glory days."

Rehabilitating the image of the morally corrupt and sleazy William Jefferson Clinton is one factor in building the momentum of presidential image for candidate Hillary Rodham Clinton. Of course, the other part of the equation is creating the dynamics that will stimulate a popular feeling that America needs a savior, and only "Saint Hillary" can descend from Mount Sinai, with tablets in hand.

Undoubtedly, the campaign whiz kids will concoct a strategy that will seek to show Hillary Clinton as an inspired and brilliant leader, with the answers to all of America's ills. Her New York senate resume will be craftily reassembled, creating a mythic image of a totally dedicated public servant, with an outstanding record of service to her constituents. New Yorkers who voted against her in the 2000 election but came to "see the light" and support her 2006 reelection as New York senator, will be paraded as converts to the cause, seeking to counter the negativity and distrust that many Americans feel towards her. Different voting constituencies will be selectively catered to, each hearing its own customized pitch from the Clintonian political machine.

All that is coarse and vulgar in American politics will be supercharged as if on steroids, fully deployed in the fulfillment of Mrs. Clinton's life-long personal ambition. A new Hillary Clinton persona will emerge out of the firmament of the airwaves and cyberspace, as though a supernatural metamorphosis from narcissistic wife of a devious and amoral politician into a celestial angel of national redemption. The American people will be subjected to a plethora of Hillary media appearances and slick advertising, all positioned to show off this new incarnation of the former First Lady.

Both Bill Clinton and George W. Bush secured their presidencies through image-creation via the media and political consultants, which was often highly dichotomized from reality. In the case of Mr. Clinton, he supposedly would be the leader to restore the American economy, after the failures of the previous president, George Bush senior. As for George W. Bush, he would restore honor and dignity in the White House, after the Oval Office degradations of William Jefferson Clinton. Thus, an absurd rationale for dynastic rule in America has been born:

1. In 1992,America needs a Clinton to undo the damage of a Bush
2. In 2000, America needs a Bush to undo the damage of a Clinton
3. In 2008, America needs a Clinton to undo the damage of a Bush.

It appears that truth really is stranger than fiction!

The record-low voter turnouts in presidential elections, combined with the bare-knuckled cynicism of the American people towards their political leaders, as attested to in numerous public opinion surveys, are demonstrable evidence that the commoditization of American politics has become antithetical to the survival of American democracy.

The process of subjecting persons of character to full and careful public scrutiny through popular elections was once considered a sacred requirement for the survival of the American republic by its founding fathers. Celebrity politics of the 21st century are the moral equivalents of dynastic hegemony and the divine right of kings to rule, the most common form of governance at the time of the American Revolution.

The thought that America could ever be ruled by a hereditary dynasty was anathema to the visionaries who founded the world's first constitutional republic. George Washington could have become a king if he wanted the title. He spurned every such opportunity as hateful to him and all he stood for. In the America of George Washington, the nation's first president had no desire to have his family succeed him in office. President Washington represented the values and ideals of the remarkable men who created the United States of America. He was learned and wise, familiar with the broad sweep of history. Virtually every nation-state that had been created since the emergence of human civilization had been ruled by family dynasties. The evidence of history was abundant to the framers of the U.S. constitution. Political dynasties, be they in the form of a Caesar or Tsar, king or queen, emperor or sultan, oppressed their citizens, stifled productivity and the pursuit of happiness, facilitated injustice and made the barbarities of war all too common a feature of the human condition.

What was most radical about the American republic in its early days was its disdain for family monarchies, and an obsession with meritocracy. In America's early days, it had its share of political scoundrels. Yet, especially in times of trial and peril, individuals of character and courage were selected as the most important national leaders by an informed and interested citizenry.

Sadly, in contemporary America, where the money of narrow and selfish business elites mixes with political lobbyists and campaign committees, a corrupt and superficial process of selecting candidates for the White House has emerged with reckless abandon. By creating Roman-like statue images of presidential aspirants, their authentic and flawed personas are transfigured into fantasy celebrity images. The result is that America may now have, by default, a virtual family-dynasty form of presidential rule. If Hillary Clinton is elected the 44th President of the United States, it will be a melancholy affirmation that the American republic, as conceived by its founding fathers, no longer endures, except in name. Two families will have come to dominate the White House, functioning as a hyphenated monarchy, for a period that may potentially encompass 28 years, or seven presidential terms.

It is only through the amalgamation of Hollywood with Washington D.C. that celebrity power has successfully demolished political substance and virtue. A celebrity image, at least within a political context, is built on fantasies and deception. In order for the unremarkable son of a Bush, or the megalomaniac wife of a Clinton, to be sent with pomp and ceremony into the White House, the American people must be subjected to mass hypnosis.

In a hypnotic state, people are vulnerable to the power of suggestion. Their natural defense mechanism, consisting of critical thinking and judicious deliberation, becomes paralyzed. They behave more like sheep than human beings, awaiting the instructions of the herder to lead them in the right direction.

Hillary Clinton will seek the approbation of the power elites, who in turn will fund her advertising campaign, for that in essence is what a political campaign is all about in America. She will be sold to the American people as though she were a bar of soap, far better that the other soap products being peddled in the form of Democratic and Republican challengers. Unfortunately, the challenges facing the American people will not resolve themselves by selecting a commoditized presidential candidate to lead the nation.

All too often, American political figures will criticize other nations for their lack of democracy. As examples, such critics will point to Syria and North Korea. In both these states, the current ruler was the son of his predecessor. Clearly, an undemocratic characteristic, giving rise to the notion that certain family dynasties regard their countries as mere extensions of the family business.

However, is it not hypocritical to criticize such political culture in other countries as anti-democratic, while remaining silent about similar trends occurring at home, in the heart of the American body politic?

If George H. Bush and Bill Clinton are succeeded as president by, respectively, George W. Bush and Hillary Clinton, how is this distinguishable from what has occurred in countries like Syria and North Korea, whose political systems we decry for their lack of democracy? What argument can conceivably be raised to refute the perception that America's celebrity politics are increasingly bearing a disquieting similarity to the path of political succession as practiced in North Korea and Syria?

The only explanation that can be offered that does not conform to the practices of acknowledged tyrannies such as North Korea and Syria is that it is merely coincidental that George W. Bush (and possibly Hillary Rodham Clinton) ended up in the White House while being the son or spouse of a previous and recent White House occupant, and the successful presidential candidate was undoubtedly the best qualified individual in all the land for such high office.

If you believe the above rationalization, then there is a bridge in Brooklyn I am eager to sell you.

Recently, a group of leading American historians concluded that George W. Bush was the worst American president, ever. Their conclusions were based not only on the Iraq war and its disastrous consequences. They also examined Bush's economic policies, which can be best summed up as borrowing vast sums of money from foreign creditors such as communist China, primarily to fund huge tax cuts for the wealthiest Americans, those whom President Bush has referred to as "my base." There is also the sad episode of Hurricane Katrina, in which the city of New Orleans, a pearl of American culture, was allowed to be virtually washed away by a storm and then ignored, while President Bush remained on vacation.

Any objective person, putting aside partisan politics, must conclude from the record that George W. Bush, if nothing else, was absolutely *not* the most qualified man in America to serve as president and commander-in-chief. To conclude the opposite is simply to abandon the historical record, deny reality and surrender to cliches and political fantasies.

Being equally objective with regards to Hillary Clinton, can one say on the basis of the information and political record that now exists, that she is the most qualified individual to assume the presidency? Restricting this question to only those identified with the Democratic Party, is she the best that this political organization can select, for presentation to the American voters in 2008?

Americans must face a painful yet critical truth, if the dangerously flawed direction the nation is currently embarked on is to be reversed.

If the people can inoculate themselves from the virus of superficial political advertising and image making, can they begin to comprehend that the system and process that selects those who should be on the front page of the National Enquirer is not the same method that should be applied towards selecting who is most qualified to serve in the White House?

The vulgarization of American politics has led the nation towards the macabre reality where its political outcomes, if not necessarily all the repressive measures, demonstrate a disturbing resemblance to societies such as North Korea and Syria. Placing the nation's fate in the hands of a Bill Clinton, George W. Bush and Hillary Clinton, however, will inflict cumulative damage on the American republic to such an extent, repression may become an inevitable destination for the people of the United States.

During the presidency of George W. Bush, his father, George H. Bush and his former adversary have become the best of friends. George Bush senior and Bill Clinton often travel together, fulfilling special tasks for George W. Bush. This bizarre camaraderie of supposed political opposites creates at least the impression of political cohabitation. A cynic might even ponder to inquire if a deal has been reached between the two families, rotating who sits in the Oval Office. Next time it's Hillary's turn, perhaps to be followed in 2016 by President Bush's brother, Jeb Bush, currently governor of Florida. And afterwards, the daughter of Bill and Hillary, Chelsea Clinton?

Foreign observers, especially among America's West European allies, have watched with stark horror and utter befuddlement what appears to be the rapid deconstruction of America' s political system, based on the notions of a strong democratic republic. Many European countries still maintain their monarchies, but for strictly ceremonial purposes. A hereditary monarch in modern Europe is devoid of even a semblance of political power. Across the Atlantic Ocean, however, what was once the most radically anti-dynastic nation on the planet has regressed to a level that would have been familiar to the potentates of the Middle Ages.

American politics has given the citizens of the United States the worst of all possibilities. By default, they now have a dual-family dynasty dominating the highest levels of national political leadership. In addition, the gene pool of the two dominating families is distinguished by mediocrity, even ineptitude, along with amorality and megalomania, as opposed to virtue and wisdom.

For this sad state of affairs, Americans can thank their media moguls, financiers and image-makers. Mixing Hollywood with Washington is absolutely *not* what the founding fathers had in mind. Reality being trumped by illusion is what led to the carnage and calamity of the Iraq war. More chilling, perhaps, is that while Hollywood can always fabricate a happy ending in a fantasy film, things do not operate like that in the real world.

Continued dominance of American politics by two monopoly parties that are hog-tied to a campaign methodology based on phony heroic images and illusionary concepts may lead to the election of Hillary Clinton as president. However, it will also lead, ultimately, to a bad ending for the American dream.

HUNDRED THOUSAND DOLLAR LADY

Maureen Dowd, a liberal columnist for The New York Times, had a fascinating conversation with a senior aide to Bill Clinton during his presidency. Discussing the First Lady, the aide told Ms. Dowd, "Hillary, though a Methodist, thinks of herself like an Episcopal bishop who deserves to live at the level of her wealthy parishioners, in return for devoting her life to God and good works."

The Republican Party makes no bones about its affection for the wealthiest Americans. They argue that cutting taxes for the rich, even at the price of borrowing from future generations of the poor and middle class, will somehow stimulate the economy for the benefit of all Americans. Even George Bush senior once described this fruitcake ideology as "voodoo economics."

The Democratic Party is more devious than the Republicans are, which is an accomplishment in itself. They proclaim publicly their disdain for granting tax relief to the wealthiest Americans, while privately licking the boots of the extreme upper class. Bill Clinton was undoubtedly a master of this double game. However, Hillary Clinton has consistently demonstrated that she is no amateur. Her affection for the personalities and lifestyle of the rich juxtaposes harshly with her pompous protestations of concern for the most disadvantaged members of American society.

Hillary Clinton demonstrated her personal priorities and values in a manner that is truly breathtaking in its illustration of avaricious proclivity, while her husband served as the governor of Arkansas. In October 1979, Mrs. Clinton made an investment of $1,000 in the commodities market. In ten months, without adding a single dollar of her own capital, she parlayed her initial outlay into a profit of $100,000. Despite having no background in commodities trading, the wife of the governor generated a return on her investment of 10,000 percent!

Commodities trading is highly technical and saturated with high risks. The trader engages in speculation on future prices of commodities such as cattle, beef and timber, purchasing and selling the commodities contracts on the same day. The short duration of the numerous transactions engaged in adds to their inherent volatility.

Not every one of Hillary Clinton's trades worked out. However, when she terminated her "career" as a commodities trader, while retaining her law job, she was clearly $100,000 ahead on an investment of a mere thousand bucks. Even experienced commodity traders would be impressed by such a remarkable return on investment.

Many years after this seemingly miraculous investment performance, the facts would emerge, which put a somewhat different tint on Hillary Clinton's foray into the world of commodities trading. As it transpired, Hillary did not have to rely on her neophyte status. She had some help from a friend of hers and Bill's. His name was James B. Blair, and besides his friendship with the Clintons and impressive knowledge of commodity trading, he was also the primary outside legal counsel for Tyson Foods Inc., one of the largest private employers in Arkansas and the nation's most substantial poultry operation.

Hillary Clinton would want every American voter to be totally ignorant of her $100,000 windfall in commodity trading during her husband's gubernatorial tenure. Failing that, she would desire that the voters swallow on blind faith the fable of Hillary being either much smarter than normal citizens are, or just plain lucky, or both.

Inquiring minds that are not blindly loyal to the contrived mythology of Hillary Clinton must delve into some disturbing correlation involving Mrs. Clinton's uniquely successful sojourn into the world of commodities trading

While Bill Clinton served as governor of Arkansas, Tyson fortuitously was advantaged by a number of state policies and decisions. This would include $9 million in government loans, appointing company executives to serve on important state boards as well as compromising on the state's environmental policies in a manner that benefited Tyson Foods.

During the Clinton presidency, Tyson would continue to benefit from policy decisions, this time emerging from the White House instead of the state house. The appearance of impropriety in the enchantment that now President Clinton continued to have for Tyson Foods would arouse sharp criticism from several members of Congress.

Hillary Clinton has never fully explained to the American public the nature of her relationship with Tyson's lead outside counsel. However, in a remarkable example of boastful and elitist candor, Mr. Blair told The New York Times during an interview conducted in March, 1994 that, referring to Hillary and Bill Clinton, "Do they have to go weed their friends out and say they can only have friends who are sweeping the streets? They have friends who are high-powered lawyers."

High powered lawyers, indeed!

From humble origins, Hillary Clinton and her husband have become fully chartered members of the landed gentry. While publicly engaging in turgid rhetoric on behalf of the poor and unfortunate, in private their time is monopolized by the people they have self-selected as their intimate friends. It is the wealthy wheel-dealers that the Clintons prefer to socialize with and establish close bonds of friendship.

Given the predilection of Hillary and Bill Clinton for the finer things of life, perhaps one can excuse their infatuation with men and women of means. After all, poor people can't buy expensive gifts.

In the closing weeks of the Clinton presidency, amid the cloak and dagger planning for last minute presidential pardons, another high priority project was under way. Hillary Clinton desired some nice things for her new home in Westchester County. The Clintons were not bashful about asking their friends to dip into their pockets, and put down for some tasteful ornaments for the Clintonian abode.

According to a news story that appeared in the Associated Press after the Clintons left the White House, "In the year before President Clinton left office and Hillary Rodham Clinton entered the Senate, the first couple received $190,027 worth of furniture and other gifts."

Though defenders of the Clintons would attempt all kinds of explanations, the simple truth was stated clearly by an unimpeachable source, who had loyally served Bill Clinton during his presidency. In an interview with NBC's Tim Russert on *Meet The Press,* Bill Clinton's former chief of staff, John Podesta, was questioned about the arm-twisting for gifts being conducted on behalf of Hillary Clinton.

Russert asked an embarrassed Podesta, "In the final weeks, did friends of Mrs. Clinton not solicit others and say, 'Would you please buy this silverware, these gifts for Mrs. Clinton for her new houses'?"

"Yes, that happened," confessed Bill Clinton's former chief of staff.

Displaying no inhibition in putting the squeeze on rich friends to ante up silverware and fine china is a remarkable display of Hillary Clinton's arrogant greed. Perhaps those of lesser means, who remain blindly loyal to her political ambitions, somehow believe that this same selfish drive is really meant to be of service to bettering America. However, what is called for is unsentimental objectivity. Seldom have politicians who have demonstrated insatiable personal and financial greed proven to be statesmen and leaders of high caliber.

Throughout history, it is the most humble and modest of persons who display heroic and wise leadership. Hillary Clinton's fascination with materialism is not an encouraging manifestation of presidential leadership potential. However, for pure hubris, her personal example is truly monumental.

Mrs. Clinton has continued her zest for good living and vast wealth acquisition even as a senator. Being a "public servant" need not mean she must work for a pauper's wage, a measly $165,000 per year as a United States senator. She had loftier ambitions to fulfill. Hillary Rodham Clinton was meant to be a literary genius, writer of best selling books.

The only obstacle to Mrs. Clinton's literary pretensions is that she apparently can't write, with the probable exception of legal briefs, while slaving at the Rose Law Firm in Arkansas. However, a turgid legal brief does not a literary masterpiece make. However, like so many other celebrities, Hillary Clinton can easily overcome this minor hurdle by hiring a ghostwriter.

Hillary's first venture in the publishing world was the self-righteous tome, *It Takes A Village.* Besides earning the First Lady cash, the book was also an attempt to soften her image, by presenting her as an "expert" on children. However, the book was almost entirely ghostwritten by writer Barbara Feinman. In what would prove a pattern for Hillary Clinton's literary products, she would not disclose on the book's cover the fact that her "masterpiece" was written by another author. Hillary Clinton's ego requires that her readers must believe that she alone was the sole author of her books.

In a shocking display of impropriety, Mrs. Clinton not only would refuse to disclose Feinman's role as ghostwriter on the book's cover, she even avoided mentioning her name in the book's acknowledgments. In what were probably among the few authentic words Mrs. Clinton wrote for her *It Takes A Village,* she indicated to her readers that, "It takes a village to bring a book into the world, as everyone who has written one knows. Many people have helped me to complete this one, sometimes without even knowing it. They are so numerous that

I will not even attempt to acknowledge them individually, for fear that I might leave one out."

However, *It Takes A Village* was small potatoes compared to the literary opportunity that came her way as her husband's presidential regime was in its final throes. In December 2000, the publishing house Simon & Schuster signed a contract with the lame-duck First Lady, providing her with a staggering advance on royalties of $8 million for her White House memoirs.

As with *It Takes A Village,* Hillary's memoirs, *Living History,* were not actually written by its supposed author. This time, a team of three ghostwriters struggled over the manuscript, seeking to present their client in the most favorable of lights, while editing out or diminishing embarrassing episodes such as Monicagate from the "history" now Senator Clinton had claimed to live. Also in harmony with her first book, *Living History* named only Hillary Clinton as the author, without acknowledging on the cover that the book's contents were, in reality, the product of other hands and minds. While Mrs. Clinton may not be the most ethical "writer" of literary works, she can not be faulted for her shrewdness in attempting to shape her image. Undoubtedly, there are many Hillary loyalists in America that are so convinced of Hillary Rodham Clinton's prowess as a writer, they may in time seek her nomination for the Nobel prize in literature.

The literary aspirations of Senator Clinton went beyond image. She was in it, as well, for the money. The publisher's advance of $8 million represented a quantum leap in the net worth of the Clinton household. Clearly, financial aggrandizement did not lag far behind her lust for power. However, a problem arouse when it was pointed out that the book deal, which was finalized after her election as New York senator and prior to her senatorial term commencing, may have conflicted with Senate ethics rules. Fortunately for Senator Clinton, Congress "polices" its own ethics controversies, meaning only seldom are those in question censured. As to be expected, the Senate Ethics Committee gave a pass to Hillary's book deal and her lavish compensation.

What is truly remarkable about Hillary Rodham Clinton's wealth enhancement schemes, aside from their entrepreneurial spirit, is her ability to pursue them in tandem with operationalizing her personal political ambitions. This symmetry with money and power is actually no contradiction, for that is how unfortunately American politics are institutionalized in our contemporary times. Given how important money is in funding political campaigns and image-making, Mrs. Clinton's innate comfort with vast wealth, and her affinity for big business moguls and investment speculators may serve her very well, as she implements her future political game-plan.

The emerging relationship between Mrs. Clinton and media tycoon Rupert Murdoch is a case in point. Mr. Murdoch, an Australian expatriate who took on American citizenship, apparently to circumnavigate U.S. rules on foreign ownership of media, is reputed to be a political conservative. His Fox television and radio network supposedly is a citadel of right-wing perspectives on public policy and current events. On the other hand, Hillary Clinton is supposedly a liberal, in terms of her politics.

What is incomplete with the above picture is that Mr. Murdoch is primarily a businessman, out to make money through his media empire. Parallel with his ambitions, Senator Clinton has her own; to become America's first female president, and also make some money along the way. In this context, political consistency is totally irrelevant. It therefore should be no surprise that the supposedly conservative Rupert Murdoch agreed to host a political fundraiser for the once liberal Hillary Clinton, in conjunction with her Senate reelection campaign.

The alignment of Murdoch with Hillary Clinton demonstrates the contrived character of political ideology in American politics. What truly counts are mutual interests among the power and financial elites in America, not political conviction. Murdoch, we can assume, is basing his decision to support Hillary Clinton on a hardheaded business rationale. If she is a front-runner candidate for president of the United States, being a strong financial backer of her political ambitions, in keeping with current American traditions, can be expected to facilitate access and influence in a future Hillary Clinton White House.

From Hillary Clinton's perspective, what counts is ambition, not scruples. As she no doubt learned from her husband, himself a consummate practitioner in the art of political inconsistency, selectively abandoning liberalism in favor of right-wing policies at suitable moments is politically expedient. Mrs. Clinton is more impressed with Rupert Murdoch's ability to raise money for her political campaigns and draw in more support from the power elites in America than his past political biography. In addition, by attracting financial support from conservative money circles, she believes she will broaden her base.

We can expect Hillary Clinton to continue to raise big money from supposedly liberal financial circles, while developing new sources of campaign revenue from such scions of perceived right-wing circles as a Rupert Murdoch. Her message may be inconsistent, though precisely tailored for each voting constituency she covets. However, she will be absolutely consistent in courting the wealthiest segments of American society. As with George W. Bush, she knows where her true "base" lies. Ever since she demonstrated an openness towards the special help she received back in 1979 that enabled her to obtain a 10,000 percent return on her commodity investment in a mere ten months, Hillary Clinton has never wavered in her affection for affluent Americans.

Many religious teachings, including the Bible, warn about money being the root of all evil. For apparently political motivations, Mrs. Clinton frequently claims that she is a pious Christian woman. She has stated publicly that she has, "always been a praying person." Perhaps what is at issue is the substance of what Hillary Rodham Clinton beseeches the almighty for.

Senator Clinton's harmony towards the financial elite in America cannot be dichotomized from the toxic influence on the corrosive deconstruction of American politics stemming from the influence of money and lobbyists. The American people are no longer surprised when members of Congress, governors and mayors are carted off to jail for acts of sordid financial corruption. With almost monotonous regularity, Americans constantly discover new examples of the brazen criminality and greed of their supposed political leaders.

In November 2005, California Congressman Randy "Duke" Cunningham, who served on the House Intelligence Committee and the Defense Appropriations Subcommittee, plead guilty to tax evasion, conspiracy to commit bribery, mail fraud and wire fraud, in a plea bargain agreement. So brazen were the acts of corruption by this Republican congressman and acute his zeal to use his committee influence to assist "clients" seeking defense contracts, he even posted a menu of services available for a set fee in bribes. As outrageous an example as this was, it has proven to be the rule for many politicians in the United States, not the exception. Though each of the two dominating political parties will proclaim itself as the corner of virtue and condemn the other as the circle of sleaziness and vice, the record shows both parties have politicians with an impressive record of abusing the trust of the American people to line their own pockets.

The recent criminal conviction of Washington lobbyist Jack Abramoff implicated senior Republicans on Capital Hill. While Democrats were gloating, simultaneously with decrying Republican corruption, one of their own was having his share of image problems.

A Democratic Congressman from Louisiana, William J. Jefferson, was videotaped by the FBI in the process of allegedly receiving a bribe of $100,000 in July 2005. Based on the videotape, the FBI executed a search warrant on the home of Mr. Jefferson. In the freezer of Jefferson's kitchen, the authorities found hidden $90,000 in one hundred dollar bills, the serial numbers matching the alleged bribery payment. The Louisiana Congressman apparently had his own unique definition of what "cold cash" constituted.

In May 2006,the FBI executed another search warrant, this time on the congressional office belonging to Jefferson. This was the first time that a law enforcement agency had ever raided a congressman's office. What followed was a reaction that told the American people everything they needed to know regarding the depths that their elected representatives had sunk to.

With the politician of one political party facing a serious corruption allegation, it would have been reasonable to expect the leadership of the other party to denounce the corruption of their political adversaries across the aisle. However, the precedent of the FBI looking at documents in a congressional office that might affirm illegal behavior was too threatening to both political parties for the usual game of partisanship. As polarized as Congress is on every other issue, miraculously, rare conformity arose out of the indignation of the leadership from both parties that the corrupt practices of some of their members might be vulnerable to more thorough investigation through the execution of search warrants on their offices.

Republican Dennis Hastert, speaker of the House, and his Democratic counterpart, Minority Leader Nancy Pelosi, issued an unusual and telling joint declaration. They both denounced the FBI raid on Jefferson's office, and demanded that the seized and potentially incriminating documents be returned in their entirety to Mr. Jefferson!

What could be more instructive of the moral failure and egregious corruptibility of the legislative branch of American government than this bipartisan effort to grant legal immunity to a member who is not exactly above suspicion, of a form that no other American citizen is entitled to?

No wonder the American people have lost trust in their political leadership, and the money-infused system that "elects" them to positions of power and privilege.

George H. Bush and George W. Bush, along with William Jefferson Clinton, were, to say the least, not exactly interested in breaking the stranglehold of money, lobbyists and corruption on the arteries of the American government. Yet, only with a president utterly committed to demolishing political corruption is there any hope of cleansing the body politic of America, and flushing out the poisonous greed that has abetted every negative trend in Washington.

The harsh truth about Hillary Rodham Clinton is that the totality of her personal and public record as governor's wife, First Lady and now senator is that she is too severely welded to the majesty of power and complicit with the money train that drives its acquisition, to become a transforming figure. Rather than drive the moneychangers out of the temple, Mrs. Clinton has given every reason to believe that she would be their heartfelt protector, and devoted accomplice.

HILLARY CLINTON'S INTELLECT

During the run-up to the New Hampshire primary in 1992, Hillary Rodham Clinton appeared alongside her husband during a prime time television interview. When questioned about why she believed her husband's suspect protestation that he was not having a romantic liaison with Gennifer Flowers, Mrs. Clinton impetuously responded, "I'm not some Tammy Wynette standing by my man."

The above quotation from Hillary Clinton provides some valuable insights on her psyche. No doubt, she did make a deal with the devil, so to speak, and abided his untruths regarding sustained marital infidelity. This applied not only to Gennifer Flowers, but other women as well, including Monica Lewinsky. However, Mrs. Clinton's reference to her not being Tammy Wynette meant that she was not some fool, blindly loyal to a cheating husband.

In fact, Hillary Rodham Clinton's remarks were indicative, perhaps unintentionally, of her willingness to put up with lies in the interests of political expediency. Essentially, she was telling not only the television audience, but also herself, that she is too smart to be a helpless Tammy Wynette. Hillary sees herself as far too brilliant to be fooled; she stood by Bill Clinton not because she believed him, but rather because her husband knew that he owed her big-time for tolerating and abiding his trysts and the deceptive gloss he poured over them.

Thus, the first manifestation of Hillary Clinton's intellectual character is a benign acceptance of deceit as a common mode of political advancement. Why tell the truth, when a lie, simple or complex, serves the immediate need of a political campaign?

During her first campaign for New York senator, the former First Lady made some incredible remarks in public, all designed to cozy up with the state's voters. For example, when apparently short of prose descriptive of such mundane matters as the federal budget, taxation and national defense, she told prospective voters that, "I've always been a Yankees fan."

Having grown up in Chicago, Mrs. Clinton had actually been partial to the Cubs. However, making a nonsensical and ridiculous claim of no substantive importance to the voters suggests the cynical disregard that Hillary Clinton has for the average citizen. A thoughtless and irrelevant claim is, in her mind, utterly appropriate to wooing the peons in her newly adopted state.

Some of the bombast that has emerged from the mind and vocal chords of Senator Clinton frankly amazes the curious observer. For example, she has actually claimed that her parents named her after the first man to climb the world's tallest mountain, Mt. Everest, Sir Edmund Hillary. The fact that this claim is contradicted by the inconvenient fact that Sir. Hillary made his sojourn to the famed mountain in 1953, six years after Hillary's birth and naming, seems inconsequential to the aspiring presidential candidate.

A clear pattern emerges from Mrs. Clinton's non-scripted verbiage, as documented on the public record, that she will apparently say anything that will advantage her political ambitions. If she will say anything, is she also prepared to do anything expedient? History warns us that such political aspirants, when connected with power, are instruments of tyranny and corrupt rule.

In evaluating the mind, character and objectives of Hillary Rodham Clinton, we must allow for the profound influence that William Jefferson Clinton has had on her development as a politician. He has been her life-long mentor, and therefore, his political standards must inevitably have a severe impact on her own political judgement.

Despite the attempts to whitewash the Bill Clinton presidency, fair-minded persons cannot deny that Mr. Clinton was a liar, on numerous occasions, and that he fibbed blatantly, with wanton indifference regarding the awkwardness and contradictions of his often-improvised fabrications. If he is Hillary's role-model and tutor, can it be any wonder that she will claim to be named after a famous mountain climber who achieved fame years after she was born? Or that she has been a life-long Yankees fan, even during her childhood in Chicago?

When you have been married to Bill Clinton as long as the senator from New York has, the normal process of osmosis alone allows for many of the ex-president's unique "qualities" to rub off and be absorbed. This then leads to a crucial question that must be raised, if Hillary Clinton's qualifications for the presidency are to be objectively evaluated. How much influence would Bill Clinton have in a Hillary Clinton White House, and would his having any influence be good or injurious for the nation?

Taking the latter point first, only a blindly loyal Clinton follower, unwilling to consider the factual record, can uphold that Bill Clinton returning to the White House alongside Hillary Rodham Clinton is a wonderful development for America. President Clinton's record as a serial liar, master of deceit and sleazy, sordid manipulation, more focussed on oral sex in the West Wing of the White House than the emerging threat of Osama bin Laden is too blatant and voluminous to ignore. George W. Bush might be a disastrous president, but restoring Bill Clinton to the White House in *any* capacity is not the prescription for the disease.

The issue of Bill Clinton's visibility alongside Hillary Clinton is undoubtedly the most vexatious strategic problem that the senator's presidential campaign advisors must grapple with. They know what is obvious to many political pundits. There is not a simple answer to the question of Mr. Clinton's involvement. With the relative success of the efforts to rehabilitate the tarnished image of Bill Clinton, there are some voting constituencies that do look on him with nostalgic favor. On the other hand, there remain many in America who will not forget the disgrace and shame he so cavalierly inflicted on the nation.

What is most telling is how Bill Clinton thought about, then deliberated on the most crucial affairs of state. This aspect of Bill Clinton's presidential record is a preview of what one could expect from Hillary Clinton as president and commander-in-chief. As with questions of politics and campaign strategy, we can expect that Hillary will continue to see her husband as a source of counsel on matters of statecraft and national security.

Perhaps the most critical threat that emerged during the Clinton presidency was the enhanced capabilities of Osama bin Laden and his Al-Qaeda terrorist organization. Before Al-Qaeda attacked two U.S. embassies in West Africa, killing hundreds, American intelligence was already briefing the president on the looming dangers stemming from Osama bin Laden. Even Bill Clinton has publicly admitted that he was informed of Mr. bin Laden's intentions to attack American targets worldwide. So, what did the 42nd president do about it?

At the time that William Jefferson Clinton was cavorting with Monica Lewinsky, the Al-Qaeda leader was in his secure sanctuary, in the African nation of Sudan. However, Osama bin Laden was perhaps not as secure as he believed, at the time. Through intermediaries, the Sudanese government communicated an interesting bargain with Washington. In return for improved diplomatic relations with the United States, and Khartoum's removal from the State Department's terrorism list, the Sudanese government would be willing to take Osama bin Laden into custody, and turn him over to American authorities.

What did Hillary Clinton's mentor and most trusted advisor do, when presented with a golden opportunity to place out of commission a sworn enemy of the United States? Nothing.

In time, sensing things were getting hot for him and his entourage, the Al-Qaeda leader left Sudan for Afghanistan, where under the protection of the Taliban regime, he planned and executed his devastating attacks on 9/11.

What possible rationalization could Bill Clinton give for such an egregious dereliction of presidential duty? At first, friends and former

Clinton officials denied there ever had been an offer by the government of Sudan to whisk Mr. Laden into American custody. When the evidence to the contrary became too overwhelming to ignore, former president Clinton was forced to admit the obvious, but put his own creative spin on reality.

Appearing before a New York business gathering February 2002, Bill Clinton said, "We'd been hearing that the Sudanese wanted America to start dealing with them again." Referring to the offer to turn Osama bin Laden over to the American authorities, Clinton continued, "at the time, 1996, he had committed no crime against America, so I did not bring him here because we had no basis on which to hold him, though we knew he wanted to commit crimes against America."

Yale-trained Bill Clinton adopted Osama bin Laden as his law client, and put the Al-Qaeda leader's interests and "rights" ahead of that of the nation to which he had taken a sworn oath to protect.

Would Hillary Clinton, recipient of the same splendid legal training from Yale's prestigious law school, have acted any differently?

What is indicative in President Clinton's public admission is the danger of having an egotistical lawyer in the White House at a time of national peril, whose only intellectual training is the intricacies of abstract legal argumentation. Hillary Clinton suffers from the same constricted intellectual thinking, in addition to having her political judgement animated by the examples of husband and mentor Bill Clinton. In addition, the times are far more perilous for American than during the two terms of Bill Clinton's presidency.

Making decisions that affect the national security and long-term interests of the United States comprise the most awesome and vital responsibilities of the occupant of the White House. Their intellectual strengths or deficits are the thin margin that separates America from the two extremes of national continuity or national calamity.

In October 1962, President John Kennedy was presented with photographic evidence that the Soviet Union had surreptitiously placed ballistic missiles in Cuba. It was the unanimous consensus of his military advisors that these missiles posed an immediate threat to America, and must be countered by air strikes and an invasion, to be mounted within days.

Had John F. Kennedy acquiesced to his military advisors, the result would almost certainly have been a Third World War, involving a nuclear exchange that would have devastated much of the planet, including the continental United States. Fortunately, President Kennedy took his own counsel, and arrived at a diplomatic resolution to the Cuban missile crisis that removed the missiles without the launching of nuclear war.

The late President Kennedy had his flaws and weaknesses, some of a personal nature, similar to what would be exhibited by Bill Clinton.

However, that is where the similarity between the two men ends. John Kennedy was not a lawyer, but had a much broader intellectual development and education, having graduated with a degree in international affairs from Harvard. He was knowledgeable about the world, and had experienced the horrors of war. Decorated for bravery during combat as a torpedo boat commander in the Pacific in World War II, John Kennedy also had a brother who was killed in the European Theatre. Kennedy came from an era when the sons of wealth and privilege were expected to lead from the front during wartime in the service of their country, and not cower in the rear.

How might the Cuban missile crisis have ended if Bill Clinton or George W. Bush had been the commander-in-chief? Even more the case with Bill Clinton, the draft dodger who lacked the ability to go toe-to-toe with his military advisors, would he have had the skill and courage to hold off his military, while rapidly coming to a creative diplomatic resolution that would safeguard the country without the resort to war? It is improbable that he would.

Based on the above perspective, every American voter must ask the question, if it had been a President Hillary Clinton facing off the Soviet leadership and her own military in October, 1962, what would have been the most likely outcome? While constructing "what if" scenarios from history is, at best, a speculative game, there are many visible characteristics regarding Mrs. Clinton's intellectual processes that give a strong hint of how she might have acted.

In a situation involving the incalculable pressures of possible nuclear war, the presidential decision-maker must be cool-headed, supremely rational, highly analytical and immune to panic. Most importantly, he or she must be devoid of impetuous thinking, for the alternative greatly magnifies the potential for war and unintended consequences.

If it had been Hillary Clinton in the Oval Office in October 1962, her previous mental training would have left her totally unfamiliar in coping with such a pressure-cooker crisis. She would almost certainly have turned to William Jefferson Clinton as her principal advisor, whose own intellectual background would only have replicated rather than augment what she brought to the decision-making table. Hillary would have consulted with her pollsters and political advisors, seeking insights on what the most politically expedient coarse might be. Being supremely ignorant of strategic and military affairs, her conversations with military advisors would have left her feeling awkward. On one hand, she would have desperately and defiantly asserted her "authority" as commander-in-chief. On the other hand, her naivete may have left her over-compensating, trying to act even tougher that the military brass.

Amidst the speculation, one thing is certain about October 1962. Most experts agree that if the president of the United States had miscalculated, nuclear war would have been inevitable, with the probable destruction of most of the nation. Substituting Hillary Clinton for

John Kennedy would have greatly enhanced the possibility of an irreversible White House miscalculation.

Is this comparison unfair to Hillary Clinton? Absolutely not. In the highly dangerous and unpredictable post-9/11 geopolitical environment, a future president may very well face a number of scenarios similar to the Cuban missile crisis. It may occur with Iran or North Korea or with China over Taiwan, or possibly Russia. Understanding how a presidential candidate would cope with an unthinkable scenario which may actually occur is a far more relevant litmus test than watching them read cute lines and talking points about non-essential issues, written by staffers.

Trying to comprehend the mind of Hillary Clinton, we see a woman of unlimited ambition and unhindered arrogance, pretending to be modest and humble. We observe a person of strident greed, acting as though she is charitable. Most tellingly, we are confronted with a personality devoid of physical and moral courage, contriving to be brave.

When Bill Clinton publicly humiliated his wife in the wake of his admission to lying about his liaison with Monica Lewinsky, it would have taken courage to speak out about her role in the scandal. A brave Mrs. Clinton would have spoken of her own pain and feelings of betrayal. She might also have expressed compassion for Monica Lewinsky, stating clearly that she was also a victim, and her husband was the sole villain in the scandal. She might have apologized to the American people for her appeal to paranoia through her earlier "vast right-wing conspiracy" tirade. She may even have left Bill Clinton, eventually divorcing him. And if she did those things, and still ran for the position of New York senator, no one could deny that she was her own woman, not riding her husband's coattails.

As history unfolded, Hillary Clinton acted in ways totally contrary to how an individual of courage, integrity and principal would have behaved. What we see is not public leadership, but private conniving. Frequently, her behind-the-scenes maneuvers have been of the pettiest character, giving further insight into the unimpressive mind of Hillary Rodham Clinton.

In 1993, the staff of the White House travel office was fired, replaced by a firm alleged to have been politically supportive of the Clinton campaign. Allegations surfaced that Hillary Clinton engineered the firings, ultimately triggering a congressional investigation involving an independent counsel. During her testimony, Hillary Clinton responded to questions with the statement, "I don't recall," at least fifty times.

In October 2000 the independent counsel finally issued his report on the matter now referred to as "Travelgate." He concluded that Hillary Clinton's testimony on her role in the firings was "factually false." Though it was determined that insufficient grounds existed for prosecution, there was nothing ambiguous about the finding that Mrs. Clinton had lied in her testimony.

In a matter as petty as "Travelgate," we find evidence of aspiring presidential candidate Hillary Clinton abusing her power for selfish and trivial ends, and then engaging in untrue statements to obfuscate her role. She may not have seduced White House interns, however, she has given rise to the feeling that she is as expedient and intermittent in her ability to speak the truth as was her husband and political mentor.

In summarizing the intellectual acuity of Hillary Rodham Clinton, we find nothing in the least exceptional about her cognitive thinking. We see, if anything, a lack of international awareness and sophistication as well as political subtlety. She has demonstrated none of the diplomatic and negotiating skills so essential for a successful presidency. Her greed, pettiness and lustful ambition are her predominating characteristics. Most importantly, she lacks any sense of a national vision or strategy that transcends her own myopic political self-interest and ambitions.

Hillary Clinton, with the enthusiastic, self-motivated assistance of William Jefferson Clinton, certainly has the ability to mount a fearsome political campaign. She will no doubt prove to be an effective fundraiser, and will assemble an efficient staff to play the political game to its finality. She will rehearse for the presidential debates, stick close to the well-researched mark and campaign slogans, and have faith that the typical superficiality of recent American presidential contests will enable her to win the game.

Should she win the game, however, the American people must be under no illusions that the mind of Hillary Clinton will prove sufficient to confronting the potentially apocalyptic challenges that await the 44th president. Senator Clinton is cunning and politically savvy when dealing with her domestic political opponents. However, should she be placed in a situation where her future adversaries include the likes of Mahmoud Ahmadinejad or Kim Jong-Il, the folly of her ambitions will truly exert their fury.

MEDIOCRITY TRIUMPHANT

Clinton's ideas electrified the audience about as much as a broken plug attached to an old land-line phone.

Larry Kudlow, Economics Editor for National Review Online, writing about Hillary Clinton's speech on the American economy, delivered to Chicago businessmen

During the 1932 presidential campaign, there could be no vagueness regarding the dire predicament confronting the American republic. A worldwide depression had devastated the American economy. A vast proportion of the American workforce lay idle. Abroad, tyrannies of the extreme left and right were proclaiming that democracy was a failure, and only totalitarian government could restore economic security.

The two main political parties understood that the issues at stake involved competing strategies for nothing less than national survival. The Republican incumbent president, Herbert Hoover, and the Democratic challenger, Franklin Roosevelt offered sharply competing yet clear visions of how to respond to a national challenge of supreme and transcending importance.

In 2008, America will again face a presidential campaign, involving two major political parties as the only serious contenders, at a time of critical challenge to the future well being of the United States. The difference, however, is that while in 1932 the campaign agendas and national conversation made it clear to everyone what was at stake, in 2008 the most vital challenges will be hidden amid a thick cloud of turgid rhetoric and banal campaign irrelevancies. Hillary Clinton and her field of White House contenders will saturate the airwaves, newspapers and cyberspace with a deadly soporific on the most pointless trivialities, barely penetrating the outer edges of the most vital issues confronting the survival of America.

Though the cast of characters and nature of national distress is differentiated from the pivotal election of 1932, there exists an important parallel criticality that is striking in its similarity to our contemporary times. As with the 1930's, these involve economic insolvency and aggressive totalitarianism.

In any debate involving the American economy, Senator Clinton is most likely to submerge her supporters in selective memory. She will look back to the last Democratic presidential administration, which coincidentally was the co-presidency of her husband and herself, as a time of plenty. She will boast of budget surpluses, unrivalled prosperity and sound economic management in contrast with the fiscal irresponsibility of the deficit-prone George W. Bush administration. In essence, her campaign strategy as it relates to the economy will be to build a romanticized and mythological epic of the Bill Clinton economy, and claim that she, as Saint Hillary, can restore the times of manna from heaven when she is restored to the White House, this time as president.

While no doubt comforting to the admirers of Mrs. Clinton, this version of the American economy under Bill Clinton's management is primarily a fable, which can be dissected and torn asunder with only limited scrutiny.

It should be recalled that the Republicans dominated both the House and Senate during the bulk of the Clinton presidency. For the most part, federal budgets and taxation policies reflected the agenda of the Republican dominated Congress. A weakened President Bill Clinton was primarily a figurehead, signing appropriations and tax bills approved by the other party, while always claiming credit when they seemed to produce positive results. His treasury secretary was a creature of Wall Street, favoring policies that inflated the value of the stock market. As we now know, much of the appreciation in American securities values was driven by crooked corporate bookkeeping, inflating earnings reports and other forms of manipulation engaged in by senior corporate management. The scandals of Enron,

Tyco and other corporate outrages became widely known during the tenure of George W. Bush, but have their antecedents during the reign of Bill Clinton.

A major source of new revenue for the U.S. government were tax revenues from the proliferation of so-called "dot-coms" during the earlier years of the Clinton administration. To a large extent, the unexpected government surpluses of the late 1990s were driven, directly or indirectly, by the so-called new economy. It was said at that time that the old business models no longer applied, specifically that one must actually make a product that consumers wanted, and sell it. A proliferation of bizarre service businesses, solely based on the Internet, with no identifiable consumer-base, was attracting vast sums of investment capital. This, in turn, generated amazing appreciation in stock prices for these new businesses after their initial public offerings or IPOs. The Clinton administration probably understood as little about this phenomenon as did the investors, but were content to be ignorant as long as they benefited from the new source of tax revenue. Despite the warning by Federal Reserve Chairman Alan Greenspan about the value of the high-tech sector of the stock market being inflated by "irrational exuberance," the record clearly shows that William Jefferson Clinton was passive when forewarned about the day of reckoning.

The reckoning did come, while Mr. Clinton was still in office. By the end of the Clinton administration, the value of high tech companies listed on the NASDAQ had declined by more than half from their peak. The "dot-com" bubble had clearly burst, wiping out trillions of dollars in capital within a short period of time, and setting the stage for a recession that began in time for the initiation of George W. Bush's administration. The Clinton high-tech meltdown and its after-affects were used as a rationalization by the Bush clique for their irresponsible tax cuts for the wealthiest Americans.

No doubt, Hillary Clinton will vociferously attack any Republican challenger for the so-called "tax relief" of President Bush. Clearly, Bush's bizarre fiscal policies have been a major factor in creating federal budget deficits of staggering proportions. Nevertheless, it must also be recognized that the policies and passivity of Bill Clinton made an equally egregious contribution towards the present perilous state of the government's finances.

With no recognized expertise in the field of economics and budget management (unless one counts her interludes with Arkansas commodities and book publishing as "business" experience), Hillary Clinton brings nothing intrinsic to the table in terms of confronting America's economic challenges. Ultimately, all she can offer is a misleading version of history. Unfortunately, fantasies and mythology are no substitute for established credentials in economics.

The myth that Bill Clinton "managed" the American economy with budget surpluses is based on the federal government keeping two sets of books. The audited accrual accounting conducted during the Clinton administration showed there was never, in fact, a budget surplus. In reality, during the eight years of the Clinton administration, the annual budget deficit typically ran into the hundreds of billions of dollars. However, as with his predecessors and the succeeding administration, the audited figures are not publicly reported to the American people. Instead, cash accounting figures are disseminated to the public and media, devoid of future Social Security and other obligations, which would be included in the audited statements, as reported by USA Today in August 2006.

If the supposed budget surplus of the Clinton administration was "cooked," then how much worse is the fiscal imbalance of the George W. Bush regime? According to USA Today, the true annual budget deficit of the United States federal government has reached the stratospheric figure of $2.9 trillion!

What neither the Democratic nor Republican parties have dared tell the American people is the painful, even terrifying yet necessary truth that America's finances are in a state of suspended calamity, verging on national insolvency. Only truth, courage and exceptional competence in a national leader can confront this hidden national emergency, and render the difficult, even dangerous radical surgery that must be undertaken to save America from imminent bankruptcy. Unfortunately, as with the incumbent president, there are no contenders as yet identified that rise to the critical needs of the nation.

As typified in Hillary Rodham Clinton, all that presently exists is mediocrity, wrapped up in shelf-worn political cliches.

Mediocrity in national leadership will ultimately lead to the bankrupting and foreclosure of America. The cumulative impact of national politicians engaging in irrelevancies, madcap adventurism and outright thievery has brought about a situation in which the *official* debt is approaching the incomprehensible figure of *ten trillion dollars*! In actuality, the true figures are even more horrendous.

Even if one were to accept the official government figures for the nation's debt, this would still come to more than thirty thousand dollars for each citizen of the United States. For example, again using only official figures, the share of the national debt tied to a family of four would be at least one hundred and twenty thousand dollars. This figure, in effect, duplicates the typical home mortgage that so many American families are familiar with. The big difference is that while the family typically pays down its mortgage every year, the politicians in Washington D.C. are adding significantly to the size of the national mortgage, with no end in sight.

Both political parties are to blame for the almost drug-induced stupor in both the White House and on Capital Hill when it comes to facing reality with respect to the American economy. Except for a small handful of the decent and courageous, for the most part politicians in Washington are unwilling to face the harsh and looming economic consequences accumulated after so many years of irresponsible public policy and fiscal mismanagement. Hillary Clinton will personify that bland inattentiveness to a fast-approaching disaster.

Vice President Dick Cheney once told George W. Bush that "Ronald Reagan taught us that deficits don't matter." Such is the level of personal denial and institutional disconnect that infests the Washington establishment. However, it would be foolish to believe that Hillary Clinton is more insightful in her understanding of economics. If she were, than Mrs. Clinton would have to denounce her own husband's presidency for collaborating with a Republican Congress in the erection of smoke and mirrors to obfuscate economic reality from the eyes of the American people.

During Bill Clinton's presidency, America's appetite for foreign energy supplies, especially oil, grew alarmingly. This led to a heightened dependency on overseas suppliers, many of them unsavory regimes. The eight years of inactivity in addressing America's energy dependency during Bill Clinton's reign were a decisive contributing factor to America's current economic vulnerabilities. With the George W. Bush administration continuing the laisez-faire energy consumption policies of the Clinton regime, the situation is rapidly forming where the chickens will come home to roost, with a vengeance.

The price of petroleum has multiplied repeatedly, within a relatively short period of time. With a lack of energy conservation policies in America, in combination with rising energy consumption in the emerging mega-economies of China and India, this trend of appreciated oil prices is likely to accelerate.

When lumped in with America's other critical economic problems, in particular the vast structural budget deficits, the likely rapid rise in the nation's energy bill does not bode well for America's future. Competing with China and India, a growing portion of the income of the American people will be diverted towards paying the family's energy bills. With the present stagnation in incomes for most Americans (but not the super-rich), a point will inevitably come when individuals will be forced by economic realities to cut back on personal energy consumption. Yet, this is not so simple. A cutback in energy consumption due to rising oil and natural gas prices will diminish other economic activity, and stifle productivity. This, in turn, will further increase the national debt.

If analyzed with logic instead of shelf-worn political dogma and ideological catch phrases, it is clear that the American economy will almost certainly, in the next presidential administration, come to a very hard landing. The decline in housing prices, which while ascendant created the illusion of national prosperity, is a clear and foreboding marker to a dark and austere future for the American people. A political establishment that has proven both uncaring and ignorant with respect to hard economic realities will only insure that a massive recession and perhaps even another great depression is an inevitable outcome.

Only an exceptionally gifted national leader, knowledgeable about economics on both a micro and macro level, would provide a brighter alternative to the bitter financial degradation that seems just around the corner for the people of the United States. However, Hillary Clinton's pending advertising and public relations campaign, no matter how thick with rhetoric or faux testimonials to her financial and economic "genius," can not substitute for her being a square peg that will never fit the required round hole.

During her first senatorial campaign in the Empire State, Mrs. Clinton boasted of her ability to restore new jobs in the wake of the de-industrialization of upstate New York. That set a predictable pattern to a pending Hillary presidential campaign. No doubt, she and her campaign strategists will chronicle job losses under George W. Bush, juxtaposed by campaign promises to add millions of new jobs to the American economy. This is a tired old campaign methodology, engaged in by all political parties. The American people have become accustomed to literally rivers of broken and meaningless promises proffered by campaigning politicians. With respect to the campaign platforms on the national economy, they have become ritualized, mere collections of manipulated statistics spiced with utopian phraseology.

The American political establishment has become so inert on matters related to the economy, there is little expectation by either the general public or more attuned constituencies that their leaders will offer sensible and well-conceived strategies for addressing America's fundamental economic challenges.

Hillary Clinton, campaign promises aside, can offer nothing more than a romanticized interpretation of Bill Clinton's economic "management." She will undoubtedly surround herself with the same Wall Street experts that her husband was so comfortable with during his two presidential terms. Without expertise or even a familiarity beyond the superficial in connection with the looming economic meltdown, how is a Hillary Clinton likely to react as things begin to implode?

In all probability, not so well. As was the case with the early period of the Monica Lewinsky scandal, it is likely that she will come up with some irrelevant oratorical diversion, to postpone the day of reckoning. A financial version of the "vast right-wing conspiracy" may become the new lexicon of a Hillary Clinton White House. Scapegoats will be sought, so that Americans will direct their anxieties and wrath in any direction other than that which points to Mrs. Clinton. There will be no FDR style "fireside" chats, rousing courage from the people and communicating in clear language what the government was planning to do.

The mediocrity of Hillary Clinton cannot be overcome by her personal ambition and political cunning. The skills that might work well to trump a political opponent are impotent in the face of global economic forces that now dominate socio-economic realties in all nations, including America. What will Hillary Clinton do about America's malignant energy dependence, as its price becomes increasingly insufferable? How will she arrest any financial panic resulting from a precipitous collapse in private real estate values, with a concomitant and catastrophic rise in mortgage foreclosures? Does she offer any solution to the continuing and escalating de-industrialization of America, other than vapid cliches?

Hillary Clinton is no Franklin Delano Roosevelt, let alone Eleanor Roosevelt. Her contrived image, phony heroism and vastly overrated expertise and questionable leadership skills leave only the paralysis of ego-driven mediocrity. In the wake of what many knowledgeable economists believe is in store for the American nation during the next several years, this is a recipe for national ruin.

One need not be a prophet of doom to clearly see the handwriting on the wall. America continues to sink deeper into a black hole of debt, with no end in sight. Only the availability of foreign credit has thus far sustained the high consumption levels of the American economy, which alone have staved-off bankruptcy. However, a point will inevitably come when foreign countries such as Communist China, Japan, Korea and the Gulf Arab states will begin to send their capital into other regions that are not as profligate in their debt-driven government expenditures.

Once foreign capital is significantly diverted away from financing the U.S. government's ever-growing mountain of debt, a pin will rupture the bubble of America's fiscal house of cards. The gigantic sucking sound that will ensue will signify for the entire world that the bubble of America's fragile economy has finally burst, and the house of cards that was the illusory edifice of prosperity will have collapsed.

A dire manifestation of America's economic deconstruction will be the catastrophic diminution in the value of the American dollar. Its artificially high value, in relation to other currencies, has been like a fiscal magnet, attracting foreign credits in the massive quantities required to finance America's profligate, debt-saturated government spending. Once the value of the American dollar is diminished to a point where it is no longer considered to be the gold-standard among currencies, foreign investors and central banks will pull their assets out of American dollar-delineated securities and debt instruments, and redirect them toward more stable economies.

The end of the American dollar's reign as standard bearer of international currencies will create a vicious circle. Declining value will chase away foreign investors, prompting even further erosion in the value of America's currency. This, in turn, will add another dimension to the rising price of foreign source energy supplies. The net effect will be a major decline in American consumption, with the spin-off effect of business bankruptcies, massive layoffs of workers, and collapse of the American standard of living. The contraction of the American economy will dry up government revenues, further exacerbating the national debt. Yet, with foreigners unwilling to extend further credit to the U.S. government, even the hallowed institution of the federal government will be left with no alternative but to shed its payroll, and dangerously reduce essential government services.

Eventually, if the above scenario plays out, a point will be reached when the American government can no longer make the interest payments on its national debt. Once this Rubicon is crossed, the United States will join a host of countries such as Argentina that have gone through the national trauma of defaulting on their foreign debts.

Should America default on its obligations to its foreign creditors, never again will it have the most powerful economy in the world. The U.S. dollar will forever be shunned as the benchmark currency of the world. The ripple effect of America's economic implosion and meltdown would scourge the entire world's economic system like a massive tsunami, inflicting social, political and economic devastation throughout the world. A global depression, not unlike that which occurred during the 1930's would lead to massive poverty and stagnation.

Beyond the economic consequences of an American financial catastrophe, there are also geopolitical after-affects to consider. Currently, the United States spends as much on defense as the rest of the world combined. In the event of a massive economic depression, this level of military spending will become unsustainable. Ultimately, America's military capacity would undergo massive contraction. Emerging mega-economies, such as China, would become the new superpowers.

Mediocre politicians are both unwilling and unable to comprehend the consequences of their failed economic policies. Hillary Clinton, by no stretch of the imagination, can even be remotely mistaken for an insightful leader with respect to the problems of the American economy and fiscal imbalance. She has given every indication that economics is not a mainstream interest of hers, beyond her own personal accumulation of wealth.

In April 2006 Senator Clinton delivered a speech to the Chicago Economic Club. The large audience of Midwest businessmen who gathered in a crowded ballroom understood what the purpose of Mrs. Clinton's oratorical exercise was all about. As one commentator who witnessed the proceeding wrote, "No doubt about it, this was the address of a presidential hopeful."

Beyond the political posturing, Senator's Clinton's speech, delivered in a cadence that would have put the most alert and energetic to sleep, was full of tired cliches from her husband's presidency. Mimicking Bill Clinton's old credo of being a "new Democrat," Hillary tacked to the right, trying to sound pro-business, while also paying homage to the more liberal wing of the Democratic Party, with unimaginative references to government activity in the national economy. The Chicago speech is a clear demonstration of Mrs. Clinton's limited view and antiquated perspective on the national economy.

In Hillary Clinton's political universe, the sole purpose of the economy as it relates to the framework of her political ambitions is to serve her campaign. Slogans that sound nice to both businessmen and minimum-wage earners will translate into more votes, so it would appear. Getting beyond the superficialities of sloganeering and cliches enters into the world of substantive and serious debate on America's massive economic problems and challenges. To do so requires integrity, courage and a high level of knowledge about economic fundamentals. It would be an act of supernatural optimism to hope that Hillary Clinton is equipped to lead us in that direction.

Hillary Clinton's flaws with respect to economic leadership are not only rooted in her ignorance beyond the superficial. Her personal and social values reflect an enchantment with the most affluent segment of American society. She and her husband are intermingled with the super-rich to an extent where their most fundamental interests are entirely mutual. Hillary Clinton will court the men and women of extraordinary means, as she seeks to raise the money required for the publicity circus that will characterize her campaign. It is therefore likely that it is to this privileged circle that a President Hillary Clinton would turn to for advice on the formulation of economic policy. These are likely to be the men and women who fill the cabinet posts that are directly tied to the economy.

The past several presidential administrations have turned to the same atypical ultra-rich in constructing the national economic policies that have led to the frightful structural problems of mounting national debt, crippling energy dependence and a widening gap between the have and have-nots. In fact, in addition to the unwillingness of the American government to pay its bills, it has abetted a growing social and economic inequality in America that defies the very essence of a just and moral society.

A noted professor of economics at New York University, Edward Wolff, has written authoritatively about the growing level of income and wealth inequality in the United States. According to his research, in 1998, while Bill Clinton was still president, the richest 1 percent of Americans owned 38 percent of all the wealth. In that same year, the top 5 percent of Americans controlled 59 percent of the national wealth. Or, as Professor Wolff stated in an interview with Multinational Monitor, "Put it another way, the top 5 percent had more wealth than the remaining 95 percent of the population, collectively."

In essence, the net effect of what George Bush senior once called "voodoo economics," which in reality is practiced by both mainstream political parties (notwithstanding their contrasting rhetoric) is to mortgage the future generations of middle and lower income Americans for the purpose of financing the greatest transfer of wealth in history into the hands of a very small but all too influential financial elite. It is a policy built essentially on greed, and therefore lacks any moral basis to overcome the inevitable arrival of the days of reckoning and judgement.

Should Hillary Clinton be elected president of the United States, it will represent the triumph of mediocrity, when only excellence can reverse America's collision coarse with economic ruin.

GODDESS OF WAR

As Israeli cluster bombs, supplied by the United States, fell on Lebanese towns and villages, killing hundreds of civilians during July 2006, Hillary Clinton spoke at a rally outside the United Nations building in mid-town Manhattan.

"We will stand with Israel because Israel is standing up for American values as well as Israeli ones," said the junior senator from New York.

What Senator Clinton would not say is if she also stood with the suffering people of Lebanon, who were caught in the middle in a confrontation between Israel and Iran's surrogate, Hezbollah. Nor would she comment on how Israel's reckless targeting of Lebanon's civilian infrastructure was somehow connected with upholding American values. Perhaps the part that she left out was her own unique conception of American values.

The above juxtaposition illustrates that the ambitious former First Lady has no well-conceived, coherent understanding of geopolitics Instead, as with so many national figures within the American political establishment, she has the usual grab-bag of cliches to pander to and appease the myriad of special interest groups and lobbyists that have come to exert a level of influence on setting American foreign policy that is unrestrained by even the most modest of mitigation.

As ominous as the looming economic challenges are for America's future, it is the disastrous trends in American foreign policy and strategic thinking which pose the greatest danger to the nation's continuity. As we have seen in an earlier chapter, the United States is mired in the brutal quagmire of Iraq, with no end in sight. Yet, Iraq is far from being the most significant external challenge to supreme U.S. national interests. However, the cost of America's intervention in Iraq is a massively dangerous distraction, which thus far has inhibited the United States from focusing on a number of far more significant external threats.

Hillary Clinton, we can safely predict, will denounce the failures of the Bush administration to confront the nuclear dangers of North Korea and Iran. As with her flaccid diatribe outside the United Nations in the summer of 2006, she will unleash an army of scripted words, framing a politically expedient foreign policy platform for her presidential campaign. By dropping the right sound bite, she will hope to "persuade" voters that she is as wise and savvy on foreign and strategic affairs as her husband had claimed to be. Perhaps, she will even draw comparisons to her husband's willingness to negotiate with the North Koreans, in contrast with the quiescent nature of the State Department under George W. Bush.

If we return to the co-presidency of Bill and Hillary Clinton, the reality appears a lot bleaker than the 2008 campaign soundtrack. In particular, the Bill Clinton administration may have negotiated with North Korea and even signed an agreed framework treaty. However, it is debatable if their North Korea policy advantaged U.S. security any more than the relative indifference of the Bush administration towards Pyongyang's nuclear weapons program.

When it first became clear that North Korea was secretly reprocessing plutonium, one of the essential ingredients for constructing nuclear weapons, President Clinton noisily pontificated that the North Korean regime would not be allowed to obtain such an arsenal. There were even hints that the Pentagon was planning a series of air strikes on North Korean nuclear facilities. However, all the tough talk and belligerent rhetoric seemed out of place in the White House of William Jefferson Clinton.

What actually ensued was an agreement between the U.S. and North Korean regime, facilitated by former president Jimmy Carter, who flew to Pyongyang and dealt directly with one of the most tyrannical regimes on earth. Ostensibly, the agreement suspended North

Korea's reprocessing of plutonium, in exchange for free deliveries of oil, pending the construction of two nuclear reactors for the regime, to be financed by America's Asian allies.

On paper, it would appear to be a better result than that obtained by the George W. Bush administration, which suspended oil deliveries, providing a pretext for North Korea to drop out of the nuclear non-proliferation treaty, and resume plutonium reprocessing. However, closer scrutiny would reveal that the Clinton framework agreement with North Korea was so severely flawed, it in no way mitigated American national security concerns. In the long-term, the agreement's loopholes and ambiguities proved a strong encouragement for the despots in Pyongyang to continue with a covert nuclear weapons program, amidst the false belief by the Clinton administration that the danger had been eliminated.

For one thing, while North Korea agreed to "suspend" plutonium reprocessing, it was permitted to retain the plutonium it had already acquired, with no safeguards or inspections. In fact, it was assumed by the American intelligence community, while Bill Clinton was president, that the North Koreans had probably fabricated two atomic bombs. The treaty, which Bill Clinton negotiated with Pyongyang, placed no restrictions on this activity, in effect consigning to the ash can of history President Clinton's onetime bellicose boast that he would "never permit North Korea to have nuclear weapons."

In addition to placing no restrictions on the use of plutonium already reprocessed, the agreement's most egregious flaw was to take North Korea at its word that it was abstaining from conducting further nuclear weapons development, and not insist on any regime of inspection. The reason this loophole was so negligently dangerous to American national security is that it left no means to inhibit North Korea from utilizing the second methodology of building nuclear weapons, namely uranium enrichment.

It appears that the Clinton administration was so self-congratulatory on its apparent success in suspending plutonium reprocessing in North Korea, it displayed an incomprehensible level of intellectual myopia in completely disregarding the possibility that North Korea would cheat on the agreement, and find ways to enrich uranium for further nuclear weapons development.

Not long after Bill Clinton left office, the U.S. intelligence community uncovered irrefutable proof that North Korea was cheating on its signed agreement with America, with almost gleeful blatancy. Specifically, the North Koreans had entered into an arrangement with Pakistan's notorious A.Q. Khan and his network, comprising a vast nuclear weapons technology black market. American reconnaissance assets, including spy satellites, revealed photographic evidence that Pakistani Air Force transports were making mysterious shuttle flights to North Korea. It soon transpired that the A.Q. Khan network had brokered a uniquely entrepreneurial arrangement between the two countries, one of which was supposedly an ally of the United States. In exchange for North Korea's missile technology and parts, the regime in Pyongyang received Pakistani centrifuges, which could be used for only one purpose. That single utility of the centrifuges involved enriching uranium. North Korea's undisclosed attempt at uranium enrichment would serve as an alternative method for building nuclear weapons, and flatly contravened the Clinton administration's framework agreement, as well as the United Nations nuclear non-proliferation treaty, or NPT, both of which the North Koreans had signed and solemnly pledged their word on strict adherence. Unfortunately for the American people, the Clinton negotiators placed far more faith in the word of the North Korean tyranny than in creating verification means that were impervious to cheating.

The George W. Bush administration certainly does not get a pass on its North Korean policy. Its passivity has provided a pretext for Pyongyang to walk out on its NPT obligations. It has resumed its reprocessing of plutonium and is, year by year, building an expanding nuclear arsenal. More ominously, the North Koreans, who apparently play by different rules than those adhered to by the mainstream international community, have provided hints that they would consider selling some of their plutonium to the highest bidder.

The failure of Bush's policy on North Korea has provided a golden opportunity for Hillary Clinton to jump into the fray, criticizing the administration while uplifting her supposed hawkish credentials on national security. These failures are compounded by an inability to thwart Iran's expanding nuclear research endeavors, which has all the hallmarks of a weapons program.

In a speech delivered at Princeton University in January 2006, Senator Clinton said, "I don't believe you face threats like Iran or North Korea by outsourcing it to others and standing on the sidelines."

Thus, a linchpin of Hillary Clinton's foreign policy platform for her evolving presidential drive had been created. Unlike George W. Bush, she will not "outsource" America's security concerns vis a vis North Korea and Iran. By inference, she will replicate her husband's supposedly more effective policies regarding Iran and North Korea. However, as we have already observed, the record of Bill Clinton's administration on North Korea was not quite as advantageous as the former First Lady would wish Americans to believe.

What about Iran? It was while Bill Clinton was president, emasculating the CIA's human intelligence capabilities, when Iran began building up what bears all the hallmarks of a massive project for acquiring nuclear arms. This activity was going on right under the noses of the politicians in Washington D.C. It would only be after the Clintons left Washington for New York that the full extent of the ambitious activities of the Iranians in nuclear research would be revealed.

Natanz is the site of an Iranian facility of strategic importance. The vaunted intelligence assets of the U.S. government never uncovered it. It would be left to an anti-regime dissident group in Iran to warn the world of what was unfolding there. Apparently, as with North Korea, the Iranian government was also an important client of the A.Q. Khan network. It was through that network that Iran surreptitiously obtained centrifuges, for the sole purpose of enriching uranium. The facility at Natanz was a top-secret installation, until its premature disclosure, that had been constructed entirely underground, said to be impervious to any attack except with nuclear weapons. It was to this vast subterranean facility that the Pakistani centrifuges were sent for installation, eventually forming cascades capable of highly enriching uranium to weapons grade standards.

Though the Iranian authorities have consistently denied that they are developing a nuclear weapon, claiming instead that they are merely working on the exploitation of "peaceful" nuclear energy, no one with any expertise on the matter believes them, or takes their assurances at face value. Their own behavior contradicts their pacifist protestations.

If the Iranians are to be believed, they only want to master the nuclear fuel cycle, so they can supply future nuclear power reactors, without being dependent on foreign sources. There are several problems with this rationale. With secure sources of processed uranium widely available, enriched to reactor standards but unusable for nuclear weapons, it doesn't make economic sense, unless the Iranians had at least 20 functioning nuclear power reactors in operation, to develop their own enrichment capability. At present, however, they are expected to have only a single such facility in operation by 2007. No further nuclear power reactors are under construction, probably due to their vast cost and long period required for construction, while Iran is presently well endowed with oil and natural gas, suitable for economically generating domestic electricity. If, however, the Iranians decided to construct 20 nuclear reactors for power generation, it would take at least 30 years, and probably longer, to accomplish this.

Clearly, based on rational analysis, the Iranian claims about its uranium enrichment project merely being for generating electricity appear to be set forth strictly for public relations purposes. However, due to the vast effort being expended by the Iranians for the creation of these facilities and their attempt to keep this activity covert in violation of the NPT agreements that they had promised to adhere to, it must be assumed that the Iranians have been trying to deceive the world as to the true purpose of their nuclear program.

A full-fledged nuclear weapons program is the only logical explanation for the massive Iranian effort to develop the technology to enrich uranium in vast quantities, in underground facilities impervious to conventional attack by aircraft or missiles. Why else would the Iranian government risk international sanctions, and turn down offers for secure supplies of reactor grade nuclear fuel from the West and Russia?

One other factor that buttresses the argument that Iran has the goal of developing indigenous nuclear weapons is their other high-priority research project. Iran has been cooperating with North Korea in developing ballistic missiles. The correlation is quite clear. Nuclear weapons are only useful if an effective means of delivery exists. Ballistic missiles serve as the ultimate method of launching a nuclear attack. Should Iran succeed, with North Korean help, in developing ballistic missiles with intercontinental range, and arm them with nuclear warheads, they will have the potential to threaten the United States with annihilating devastation.

If North Korea helps Iran build missiles that could strike American targets, it stands to reason that Pyongyang, as with Tehran, will also arm its intercontinental delivery systems with atomic warheads.

The nuclear threat presented by Iran and North Korea, along with the possibility of international terrorists acquiring weapons of mass destruction, poses the single greatest threat to the very existence of the United States. Without question, the geopolitical and strategic ineptitude of the George W. Bush administration has severely enhanced America's vulnerabilities to these dangers. The question is, would a President Hillary Clinton perform any better?

The New York senator's scripted words delivered at Princeton, along with her monotone pandering at rallies organized by special interest groups, do not provide for an encouraging answer. Most likely, she will compare Bush's ineptitude and dogmatic stubbornness with the supposedly more pragmatic posture of her husband's administration. As we have already observed, however, the vaunted agreement that the Clinton administration negotiated with the North Korean dictatorship had more holes than Swiss cheese.

One of the most daunting obstacles to addressing the Iranian and North Korean nuclear challenge is lack of accurate intelligence. Relying on a president's instinct, in the absence of verifiable intelligence information, is not a prudent course or policy for a nation to follow. George W. Bush's "instinct" on Iraq's supposed possession of WMDs harshly demonstrates the frailty of human subjectivity. The same could be said for William Jefferson Clinton's decision to refuse an offer from Sudan to turn over to American custody Osama bin Laden.

Given President Bill Clinton's poor performance with respect to the effectiveness of the American foreign intelligence apparatus, especially with regard to human sources and methods in target countries, it would be a blind leap of faith to expect a radically improved posture from his wife. Furthermore, the danger is so acute and imminent, there may not be nearly enough time to rebuild the CIA and other intelligence assets degraded by Bill Clinton, and not significantly rehabilitated by President Bush.

Given the stark dangers accumulating from North Korea and Iran, it will fall to the quality of strategic thinking, wise judgement, judicious counsel and innate knowledge of the person elected president in 2008 to insure that America can navigate the turbulence and minefields which lie ahead. Hillary Rodham Clinton's PR machine and campaign speechwriters can in no way compensate for her glaring deficits in all these critical areas of leadership.

Focussing on Iran, the next president will face a horrific set of possibilities. Given that Iran is almost certainly engaged in a frantic drive to build nuclear weapons, what would be the correct response? George W. Bush claims that, like Bill Clinton on North Korea, he will not tolerate an Iranian nuclear weapon being developed. And, as with North Korea, that is apparently what is occurring, notwithstanding the presidential rhetoric.

Despite Bush's rhetoric, he apparently decided to focus on what he perceived to be an "easy" target, Iraq, while ignoring the two other members of his self-defined "axis of evil." Aside from rhetorical flourishes, it appears that Bush is placing America's future in the hands of a controversial missile defense shield.

The supposed missile defense shield, a scaled-back version of Ronald Reagan's "star wars" concept of the 1980's, is a hideously expensive technological white elephant, which many experts believe will never work. It is, in effect, an electronic version of the Maginot Line that France constructed before the Second World War, to ward off a Nazi invasion. Bush's 21st century Maginot Line is probably fated to be as ineffective in protecting America.

A growing number of Washington and Pentagon insiders have expressed their views to the media, suggesting that it is inevitable that Iran will become a nuclear-armed state, and rather than attempt to prevent this from occurring, America should focus on containment strategies, as with the Soviet Union during the Cold War. Unfortunately, an important element within Iran's ruling theocratic elite harbors extreme Shiite Islamic religious views about the ultimate confrontation between it and "satanic" America that are unlikely to be deterred or altered by the thought of mutual assured annihilation, as was the Soviet Union of old.

Iran, however, is a complex geopolitical space. Even within the Iranian religious autocracy, there do exist more rational elements that primarily want to preserve their hold on power, and see nuclear weapons as a deterrent to what America inflicted on Saddam Hussein and Iraq. The American failure to respond decisively to the North Korean nuclear threat is probably seen by these Iranian leadership circles as validating the utility of becoming a nuclear-armed state. In addition, there is the wider Iranian society, which prefers normalization of relations with America, rather than permanent confrontation, let alone an apocalyptic embrace.

Given the complex configuration of political forces at work in Iran, how would a President Hillary Clinton act and what would be her policy? She has given few clues, preferring to see this vital question as merely another opportunity for her to engage in political posturing and polemics. While deriding the Bush administration for "outsourcing" the diplomacy on Iran and North Korea, she has otherwise issued forth the same vapid and inert verbiage. As with Bush, she would call for sanctions. In her Princeton speech, Senator Clinton said, "we must have more support vigorously and publicly expressed by China and Russia, and we must move as quickly as feasible for sanctions in the United Nations."

By any standard, Mrs. Clinton's words cannot be taken as evidence of a knowledgeable person of state engaged in serious and insightful strategic deliberation. She merely pontificates with the same taglines that are indistinguishable from most Washington politicians, be they classified as Democrat or Republican. Such superficiality on the part of the next American president may lead to egregious miscalculations, setting in motion a chain of events that will likely facilitate a level of destruction and carnage that will make Iraq look like a schoolyard fight.

The president of Iran, Mahmoud Ahmadinejad, is on record as expressing hope that the United States will one day cease to exist. If Iran were to have nuclear weapons, would he then act to translate his hopes into reality, disregarding the retaliatory consequences that are likely to ensue? Having a U.S. president that can make a correct diagnosis on this question, factoring in all the other complexities of Iran's political culture, will prove crucial for the maintenance of world peace.

Hillary Rodham Clinton's long record shows personal ambition and greed, and skill in defeating political opponents. However, there is not a shred of convincing evidence that demonstrates that she has developed a high level of sophistication towards understanding Iran, the nature of the threat it poses and the opportunities and strategies to effectively cope with the challenge.

At times, Mrs. Clinton has referred to Iran's threats to Israel, pandering to the pro-Israel lobby, a source of campaign contributions and votes. This mimics the narrow-minded expediency that so characterized the presidency of William Jefferson Clinton. However, the junior senator from New York has failed to articulate a clear strategic vision on how Iran's attempt to acquire nuclear weapons capability threatens the United States in a fundamental manner. Perhaps the lack of any immediate political benefit does not justify the intellectual effort, from her perspective.

The overarching danger of Iran's nuclear program will require a grand strategic approach, incorporating all the elements of diplomacy, economics, intelligence and military preparation and doctrine. All the assets of American power and projection will need to be harnessed in an unprecedented way, to ward off disaster, at home and abroad. An important component of a grand strategic approach will involve having a president who will go beyond the typical Washington insiders for advice, and seek out the counsel of America's scholars, professional diplomats, intelligence officers and journalists who have deep knowledge about Iran, it's political dynamics and divisions.

A president with the wisdom to construct a grand strategic approach towards dealing with Iran will maximize the opportunity of eliminating the danger to America of an Iranian nuclear arsenal without resort to acts of war, while simultaneously initiating a process that brings about the eventual normalization of relations between the two nations.

The former First Lady does not arouse confidence that she has the intellectual capacity and moral courage necessary to construct a sophisticated, highly substantive grand strategic approach towards resolving the Iranian nuclear challenge. Therefore, should she be elected president, how might she deal with Tehran?

A future President Hillary Clinton may decide to follow the model her husband established in addressing the North Korean nuclear issue. By any objective criteria, that was a dysfunctional model, despite Clintonian propaganda. Nevertheless, it is certainly possible that Mrs. Clinton would rehabilitate the framework agreement of Bill Clinton as a solution to the Iranian crisis. However, not only would it be as flawed and saturated with loopholes, as was the case with North Korea. It is likely that even a Munich-like overture to the Iranians would be rejected, unless it allowed them to continue with the enrichment of uranium, which leaves their capability to develop nuclear weapons intact.

What Hillary Clinton may find difficult to grasp is that Iran is a fundamentally different challenge then that which Bill Clinton encountered with North Korea Tehran has given every indication that its vast investment in creating the industrial infrastructure required for uranium enrichment is the single most important national priority for Iran's leadership. The Iranian regime has provided ample affirmation that it will not reverse its colossal expenditure in developing a nuclear weapons capability merely for assistance in building a few peaceful nuclear reactors, and receiving the fuel to make them operational.

If the White House is led by a commander-in-chief with a broad strategic vision, it will come to terms with the core issues that underlie Iran's decision to embark on a full-scale effort at developing nuclear capability, in spite of the risks of economic sanctions that Senator Clinton frequently and shrilly advocates. How Washington interprets those issues, and the correctness of its judgement, will determine if a peaceful and comprehensive resolution to the Iranian nuclear issue can be secured.

During Bill Clinton's presidency, there was actually the possibility of a thaw in relations between the U.S. and Iran. Ahmadinejad's predecessor, Mohammad Khatami, served two terms as a popularly elected reformist president of Iran. His power severely curtailed by the religious establishment and its hard-liners, Khatami made many overtures to the United States. If Hillary Clinton's husband had demonstrated wisdom and a sophisticated comprehension of Iranian politics, he could have engineered a major rapprochement that would have enabled the reformist movement to prevail in Iran, reducing and perhaps eliminating the threat of a nuclear confrontation.

Unfortunately, Iranian-American relations were not a priority of Bill Clinton's. He preferred to invest the time he devoted to foreign affairs in wooing Yasser Arafat, the corrupt leader of the Palestine Liberation Organization. Eventually, after Clinton left office, the Palestinian people would elect the hard-line Hamas movement to head their government, as an expression of their disgust with the cronyism and corruption of Arafat's PLO.

During Bill Clinton's administration, Arafat received more invitations to visit the White House than any other foreign leader. Even Hillary Clinton became involved in the cultivation of Yasser Arafat. During a visit to the West Bank, she publicly embraced Suha Arafat, the PLO chairman's wife, who reputedly received tens of millions of dollars from PLO funds to subsidize her lavish lifestyle.

In retrospect, it appears bizarre that the Clintons were so disengaged on Iran, but obsessed with the personality of Yasser Arafat. Perhaps the only explanation is that Bill Clinton was more concerned with his legacy, and believed that if he developed a rapport with the PLO leader, he could convince him to sign an agreement with Israel that would land him the Nobel Peace Prize. Such recognition might have encouraged the American people to forget about the Monica Lewinsky scandal.

The failure of the Clinton administration to comprehend the nuclear activity occurring in Iran as well as its true nature, combined with a woeful neglect of opportunities to impact Iranian society and political dynamics, have made a vast contribution to the enormous danger that now exists in the Middle East. While the inadequate response of the Bush administration to the Iranian nuclear challenge has added to the menace, Hillary Clinton's criticism of Mr. Bush is disingenuous, to say the least. She stood by, as in effect co-president, while her husband subsumed himself in trivialities and banal diversions. America may yet pay a very steep price for what Bill Clinton chose not to do about Iran during his presidency. If Hillary Clinton is elected president, that invoice will undoubtedly come due.

North Korea is the other looming disaster that the next president must cope with. We already know Hillary Clinton's public posture; terminate George W. Bush's "outsourcing" and return to the "brilliant" Clintonian diplomacy that brought about the flawed framework agreement, which we now know the North Koreans violated with alacrity. Beyond Senator Clinton's rhetoric, what would she actually do about North Korea? As menacing as the Iranian nuclear program is, what distinguishes North Korea is that it is believed to already possess a nuclear arsenal. Furthermore, Pyongyang has begun testing ballistic missiles with the range to reach targets in the United States.

Perhaps the most vital question that the next American president must resolve is deciphering North Korea's true intentions with respect to its nuclear arsenal. The post-Bill Clinton CIA does not have reliable intelligence assets in North Korea, meaning the president will have to rely, to a very great extent, on his or her own strategic and tactical acumen. If Hillary Clinton were to be the commander-in-chief, that is too much to put stock in, while facing a growing and dire threat.

The North Korean State is headed by Kim Jong-Il, son of its founder. Thus, he represents the first communist dynasty, a development that would undoubtedly have confounded Karl Marx. His country is an economic basket case, with antiquated factories forced to shut their doors and an agricultural system incapable of warding off repeated outbreaks of famine. It would appear, based on the evidence, that improving the lives of the North Korean people is not at the top of Kim Jong-Il's list of priorities. Preserving his dynastic rule, and the cult of personality that forces his people to worship him as a living God, is likely what he is most concerned with. This motivation goes to the heart of North Korea's expanding inventory of atomic weaponry and ballistic missiles.

If the administration that succeeds George W. Bush maintains the current policy, nothing concrete will be done to halt North Korea's production of nuclear bombs. A President Hillary Clinton may push for economic sanctions. However, for two presidential terms the Bush administration has also called for sanctions, with nothing actually occurring. Certainly, the North Korean regime is not intimidated by threats of sanctions. The end result will probably be the same. Pyongyang's stock of atomic bombs will continue to expand.

If the next president decides that there is nothing that can be done to convince North Korea to eliminate its nuclear weapons stockpile, then that means the nation will place its trust solely in nuclear deterrence and a likely ineffective missile defense shield. How wise a policy would that be?

The answer is probably not wise at all. The North Korean regime is fanatically strident, and notoriously immune to even the most basic norms of international conduct. For example, the North Korean government has kidnapped Japanese children in their own homeland, and secretly spirited them off to North Korea. It has committed repeated acts of terrorism against South Korea, including bombing a civilian airliner and murdering South Korean officials visiting a foreign country. It constantly sends teams of infiltrators into South Korean territory. The North Korean government brazenly counterfeits American currency, in large quantities. In effect, it acts like a state that is at war with much of the world. Perhaps most shocking, several North Korean embassies have been caught red-handed with involvement in heroin smuggling.

A country that is so economically strapped that it must require its own embassies to engage in narcotics trafficking in order to generate liquidity for the regime may see its growing nuclear arsenal as a potential cash-cow. If Iran, or even more ominously, Al-Qaeda, were to offer substantial payment for nuclear bombs or plutonium, what reason would the American people have to believe that North Korea would feel enough restraint not to go to that level? Will Hillary Clinton prefer to believe that heroin smuggling is as far as Pyongyang can go, but it will be entirely responsible in managing its nuclear "deterrent?"

Nothing that has emerged from the lips or intellect of Hillary Rodham Clinton gives any basis to have confidence in her judgement in confronting the North Korean nuclear threat. Based on the output of her husband's administration and her intimacy with its deliberations, it would be a lopsided leap in expectations to conceive of her having the strategic insight to formulate a sober and accurate estimate of the risks posed by Pyongyang's retention of a nuclear weapons capability.

If Hillary Clinton were to assume the presidency, and attempt to resurrect her husband's framework agreement, it is unlikely that anything concrete will flow out of such an exercise. As we now know that Pyongyang deliberately cheated on the original framework agreement, it is clear that they never wavered in their decision to acquire nuclear weapons. To them, putting ink on a treaty with the Clinton administration had no more solemnity than the price of the pen. It is doubtful that Hillary could obtain any agreement that would verifiably eliminate North Korea's nuclear arsenal.

If the next administration cannot obtain a diplomatic solution to the North Korean nuclear issue, then it will be faced with two very bad choices. It could follow the pattern of George W. Bush, which is to engage in rhetoric but essentially do nothing. There is also the military option. They both have more disadvantages than advantages.

By doing nothing while Kim Jong-Il continues to run his assembly line for atomic bombs runs the risk mentioned earlier, namely that North Korea will sell some of its nuclear weapons on the black market. Should that happen, it would be almost inevitable that an American city would be the site of the detonation of one of Pyongyang's devices, inserted there by a client terrorist group.

There is perhaps also another danger.

North Korea, bankrupt as it is, still abides by its ideology that South Korea must be reunited with the North, under the rule of Kim Jong-Il. If its nuclear arsenal becomes large enough, it may attempt to repeat the Korean War of half a century ago, seeking to conquer South Korea by force. If it has missiles armed with nuclear warheads with the range to strike at the continental United States, it would probably issue an ultimatum, threatening that the United States must not intervene in North Korea's conquest of South Korea, or else see several of its major cities obliterated.

The above scenario is a terrifying glimpse into the future, but unfortunately, far from inconceivable. Given what we already know about the performance of Bill Clinton's administration on foreign and national security policy, what basis is there for America to place its trust in the mind, intellect, analytical skills and strategic insight of Hillary Rodham Clinton?

Mrs. Clinton's repudiation of what she caustically refers to as "outsourcing" as a means of handling the North Korean threat betrays her intellectual vacuity, for it is an expression of her predilection for catchy campaign phrases in lieu of thoughtful policy pronouncements. Though the Bush administration has been diverted by the Iraq war and has been lethargic and ineffective in responding to the North Korean menace, it is essentially correct that involving China is an essential component towards resolving the nuclear crisis on the Korean peninsula. What Senator Clinton derisively refers to as "outsourcing" may be the only means of effective coercion that Kim Jong-Il would respond to, if a skillful and diplomatically savvy American president understood the dynamics of China's relationship with the North Korean regime. Hillary Rodham Clinton's own vapid rhetoric is the clearest manifestation of her disinterest and lack of comprehension in connection with China's role in formulating a resolution of the North Korean nuclear question that would spare the American people a future clouded by darkening danger and chilling uncertainty.

Iran and North Korea pose immediate flash points that the next president must deal wisely and effectively with. Yet, they are not the only threats of macabre proportion hovering over the American people, like the sword of Damocles. Perhaps the most sinister danger of all is the potential nexus of transnational terrorist movements armed with weapons of mass destruction. This is an area where Hillary Clinton's suitability for presidential leadership must be subjected to the most severe scrutiny, for the consequences of failure and flawed judgement could be apocalyptic.

The administrations of Bill Clinton and George W. Bush have both proven malignantly deficient in addressing the threat of radical Islamist terrorism, especially with regards to the acquisition of nuclear weapons. Al-Qaeda's leader, Osama bin Laden, has been consistent and clear in his intentions to obtain and use nuclear bombs. The obvious targets of his atomic nightmare fantasies are major urban centers in the United States.

While Bill Clinton was serving his two terms as president, the former Soviet Union underwent a prolonged period of chaos and anarchy. During this period of instability, it was recognized by leading American national security experts that the vast but poorly secured stockpile of what had been the Soviet Union's nuclear weapons and fissile materials (plutonium and highly enriched uranium) were dangerously vulnerable to theft by Al-Qaeda, or black market criminals who would sell to international terrorist organizations for the right price. Two courageous and thoughtful American senators, Republican Dick Lugar of Indiana and Democrat Sam Nunn of Georgia, led a bipartisan effort to enact legislation that provided American financial assistance to upgrade vulnerable nuclear weapons and nuclear materials sites in Russia. By denying access to these materials by nefarious groups such as Al-Qaeda, the single most important step in protecting America from a future nuclear 9/11 was undertaken.

Unfortunately, neither Bill Clinton nor George W. Bush were fully engaged in pushing through the implementation of this essential program. As a result, in the more than ten years that the program has been underway, only half of the vulnerable nuclear sites in former Soviet territory have had their security sufficiently upgraded. It is estimated that unless the program first established by Nunn and Lugar is pursued far more energetically, it will take at least 12 more years to complete.

Hillary Clinton has thus far given no indication that she has internalized America's vulnerability to the apocalyptic danger of nuclear terrorism. Senator Clinton has offered no substantive policies or solutions toward mitigating the threat posed by Al-Qaeda and its desire to acquire the means to inflict mass destruction on American soil. Her lack of outspokenness on the issue defines the marginal priority such a looming danger has within her political universe, notwithstanding her claims to be concerned with homeland security ever since thousands of her constituents were massacred on 9/11.

The record of her husband's presidency, when she functioned as effectively Bill Clinton's co-president, does not provide a basis for encouragement that Hillary Clinton would be an effective commander-in-chief in decisively leading America's fight against the terrorist threat posed by Islamist radicals. In addition to Bill Clinton's egregious lethargy in responding to the growing threat of Al-Qaeda, Mrs. Clinton has given ample evidence that her own political self-interest has inhibited her ability to comprehend the vital role of relationship-building between America and the Arab world has in enhancing American security.

When Hillary Clinton unleashed her torrent of pandering vocabulary to a rally representing supporters of pro-Israel lobbying organizations, she gave persuasive evidence that courting the Jewish vote was more important to her than framing a balanced foreign policy for the Middle East that would support Israel's security, without negating legitimate Arab interests and concerns. The perception that the United States lacks balance in the Arab-Israeli dispute, which proliferates throughout the Arab world, has served to undermine America's allies in the region, while stimulating recruitment for radical organizations that adhere to the ideology of Osama bin Laden.

Senator Clinton's speech to a partisan rally representing the pro-Israel lobby is reflective of her innate lack of moral courage and grasp of geopolitical realities as they impact the Middle East. When Hillary Clinton linked Israel's aerial bombardment of Lebanese towns and cities with the "defense" of American values, she was facilitating an image in the Arab world that those values are hostile to their own culture and dignity. Not surprisingly, such negative image-projection as engaged in by Mrs. Clinton only succeeds in further alienating the 320 million people who inhabit the Arab world from positive feelings toward the United States.

An inseparable component of any effective strategy geared towards marginalizing the Islamist terrorist threat to American interests abroad, as well as the homeland, is enhancing the image of the United States throughout the Arab world. Hillary Rodham Clinton has thus far demonstrated that her narrow domestic political self-interest negates the broader understanding and strategic comprehension that would suggest the level of leadership acumen required to initiate and sustain such a policy. At a time when most of America's allies decried Israel's disproportionate response to a Hezbollah cross-border raid, the former First Lady reveled in being a cheer leader for the Israeli governing political party. Even many Israelis, and a large portion of the Jewish-American community, were not blindly supportive of Israel's military attacks on Lebanese civilian targets, in contrast with New York's junior senator.

The above mode of behavior on the part of Hillary Clinton seems to reinforce the view of her as being a human being who is politically expedient, even at the expense of fundamental American national interests. In this affectation, she does not distinguish herself in the least from her husband and mentor, a proven master of expediency. The presidency of William Jefferson Clinton reeked of political expediency and opportunism. By demonstrating that she is virtually a Siamese twin of her husband's in the conception of politics and policy formulation, Mrs. Clinton should arouse grave reticence on the part of the American people.

A mindset that is subsumed with notions of political opportunism, and most comfortable in espousing non-substantive cliches for the purpose of cultivating domestic political constituencies, stands in contradiction to the requirements of inspired and visionary leadership. If a person as bereft of leadership skills and moral courage as Hillary Clinton does become president and commander-in-chief, what are the possibilities that world peace will be secure? In the geopolitical context and security architecture that currently exists and as previously outlined, the odds are not favorable.

Electing Hillary Clinton as president in 2008 will make it far more likely that the United States will face an enhanced risk of war, on multiple fronts. In a worst-case scenario, the very continuity of the United States may be placed in jeopardy by a second Clinton presidency.

Some American politicians have drawn parallels to 1939, when the policy of appeasing Fascist dictators by the democracies of Western World brought about the Second World War. Typically for U.S. political figures, this is theatrical oratory. In fact, there is a historical parallel that is far more relevant to the current period; Europe in 1914.

In the months preceding World War I, the world appeared to be at peace, with Europe and America experiencing an unprecedented level of prosperity and scientific progress. Yet, underneath the facade of disquieting calm, immense and turbulent storm clouds were gathering.

As with the phenomena of terrorism today, much of Europe and even America was plagued by outbreaks of terrorist violence, under the guise of the anarchist movement, Balkan nationalists and extreme socialists. The other parallel with present times is that Europe, in particular, was governed by a largely inept coterie of leaders, many of them part and parcel of dynastic rule, as with the Kaiser in Germany and Tsar in Russia.

A single act of violence by Serbian terrorists in the summer of 1914, resulting in the assassination of the heir to the Austro-Hungarian throne and his wife, should never have sparked the conflagration that became the First World War. However, over a period of several weeks, the bumbling ineptitude and miscalculating stupidity of many of Europe's mediocre rulers brought about a war that nobody in their right mind would have desired. The results were ten million dead, widespread devastation, and lingering resentment that brought about the Second World War, with another fifty million dead. Except for the final act at Hiroshima and Nagasaki, this was a bloodbath brought about with conventional arms.

If the world's sole super-power is in fact transitioning the 21st century's parallel to August 1914, the consequences of having a president and commander in chief who lacks the intellectual fortitude required to avoid miscalculation may be a far more horrific tragedy than occurred nearly a century ago. Given the constellation of geopolitical and transnational phenomena of a threatening character currently unfolding that threatens America, nothing short of exceptional national leadership can secure America's security and peaceful coexistence with the world.

The former First Lady had eight years of schooling in national governance and leadership from a man of expediency, vulgarity and lustfulness. Bill Clinton, whatever his other talents may be, can certainly not be held as a role model for being a wise helmsman in the current state of world tension and stormy diplomatic weather. Given the paucity of any other form of education in the areas of statecraft, strategy and international relations that Mrs. Clinton has had the opportunity to absorb, it is unfortunately to the model of Bill Clinton that she can be expected to look to, and issuing forth her presidential decrees in areas involving national security.

As with her husband, a President Hillary Clinton is likely to select a personality that she is comforted by, as her most trusted and senior advisor on issues involving the national security of the United States. Especially when the president is unschooled in the intricacies of national security, strategy and geopolitics (notwithstanding grandiose claims to the contrary in campaign advertisements), the success of his or her administration in preserving peace and enhancing the security of the nation in large measure depends on the person that is selected to be the national security advisor.

In several instances, presidents chose national security advisors who had highly recognized credentials in the complex field of geopolitical strategy. Henry Kissinger, who served as Richard Nixon's national security advisor, was a highly respected Harvard academic in the field of geopolitics and security issues before his presidential appointment. He was widely published in the field of national security matters, including the question of nuclear arms.

What about the man that Bill Clinton selected to be his principal advisor on national security matters? Given his own paucity of knowledge on this intricate yet vital area of presidential responsibility, this was clearly a presidential appointment of immense importance.

In the period 1997-2001, Mr. Clinton's national security advisor was Sandy Berger, having previously served his boss as deputy national security advisor. Mr. Berger was a lawyer, who lacked the level of scholarly credentials in national security matters that were characteristic of Henry Kissinger. It would appear that his main credential for the job was that he had been a longstanding friend of Bill Clinton, dating to the time they were both involved in George McGovern's presidential campaign of 1972. It was on Sandy Berger's watch that America responded ineffectively to Al-Qaeda's growing threat to America. The miscalculations in handling the nuclear challenges posed by Iran and North Korea, as outlined above, were also formulated by the Clinton administration while Sandy Berger was a principal source of advice and counsel on national security matters.

As national security advisor, Mr. Berger had CIA analyst Mary McCarthy appointed to a senior intelligence position at the National Security Council. The CIA would subsequently fire Ms. McCarthy in April 2006, following a polygraph examination, in connection with the leaking of classified information to the media.

In 2004, the U.S. Justice Department initiated an investigation into the mishandling of classified material by Mr. Berger. At first, Berger claimed he had unintentionally and accidentally removed classified materials from the national archives. Subsequent investigation, however, led to a very different determination. In April 2005 Sandy Berger plead guilty to the unauthorized removal of classified documents.

No better epitaph can exist to explain the caliber of the man that Bill Clinton selected as his most trusted advisor in protecting America's security interests.

Hillary Clinton's assumption of presidential power, while being largely ignorant of the questions that involve the most fundamental aspects of U.S. national security, is a prescription for calamity. Following the example of William Jefferson Clinton in relying on national security advice that does not meet the highest standards will only serve to magnify the probabilities that any administration she heads will blunder into disastrous miscalculations.

All the evidence and public record thus far defines Hillary Clinton as a politically expedient actor, in synchronicity with her husband and mentor. While such expediency has enabled her to be elected twice to the Senate, and may bring her back to the White House, it is totally antithetical to providing the quality of wise statesmanship that will be essential for America's survival in the 21st century.

In 2008, the American people must find the courage to transcend the illusions created by campaign rhetoric and vulgarity, and reach a sober and well-informed judgement on who will be most qualified to lead the nation during perilous times, understanding the consequences of poor presidential judgement. The bloody quagmire of Iraq may be but a harbinger of much worse to come, unless a person of character, wisdom and worldly knowledge and sophistication serves as America's next commander-in-chief.

Given the constellation of storm clouds gathering on the horizon of the new century, having a mediocre and politically ambitious megalomaniac figure making the key decisions of state is an alignment with catastrophe. It is also a rash gamble with history. If, indeed, the contemporary world resembles the apocalyptic dynamics that existed in the summer of 1914, then the admixture of nuclear armaments portents a cataclysm that will be vastly more devastating to humanity.

Mrs. Clinton may seek to distract the American electorate from her grave human deficiencies and deficits with respect to protecting America's security interests. Undoubtedly, there are ample resources available to assist her. Through the wealthy elite that she is attuned to, she will raise massive amounts of money, financing an undoubtedly clever multimedia campaign. The cascade of sound bites, thirty second scripted cameo appearances and negative attack ads will, however, be silent on what her credentials and qualities really are that would justify 300 million Americans entrusting their lives to her decision making.

If Hillary Clinton seriously believes that she is the most qualified person in the United States to serve as commander-in-chief at so crucial a time in American history, there are concrete steps she could take to make her case. Dispensing with speeches to elite groups, where she would merely read the text of policy papers written by minds other than her own, she could choose to address televised town hall meetings, without the benefit of a written text. Talking to the American people extemporaneously, she could attempt to articulate her viewpoint on the current international situation, and what her approach would be in response to the most critical challenges that confront the nation.

An honest exposition by Hillary Clinton on her geopolitical Weltanschauung is unlikely to occur during the 2008 campaign. To do so would be to demolish the mythological and contrived imagery that will seek to convince the American people that an egotistical yet mediocre woman of exaggerated ambition somehow warrants their trust. In the absence of candor from Hillary Clinton on her "qualifications" for strategic judgment, the American people must circumvent the public relations blind alley that her campaign machine will spin, and objectively judge Mrs. Clinton's leadership acumen for themselves. There is too much at stake to rely on media circuses and hype, celebratory name recognition and clever campaign advertising.

In rendering a judgement on the suitability of Hillary Rodham Clinton for high office, the American people must ultimately ask themselves a sobering question: based on her prior experience, tutelage under William Jefferson Clinton, and scarcity of evidence attesting to her geopolitical acumen. That question, ultimately, is if America would be more likely to sustain peace or be plunged into war if its commander-in-chief would be President Hillary Clinton.

It is this author's view that the record of Hillary Rodham Clinton speaks for itself. Her politically expedient vote for the unnecessary and disastrous war in Iraq is a window on what her presidency would likely resemble, in any council digesting grave issues of national security. We see a person who is cunning and calculating, but not in conducting wise diplomacy or formulating sound national security policies. Rather, we see her cleverness directed towards manipulating events that benefit her personal and political self-interest. This is a mindset that can serve one person's selfish agenda, but is antithetical towards providing skillful and inspired leadership in tumultuous times for an entire nation.

In the cases of President George W. Bush and his predecessor and Hillary's husband, Bill Clinton, we can see how presidents who wield America's power with a lack of strategic wisdom and geopolitical awareness can inflict grave damage on the nation's security and safety. The appalling example of Iraq is a solemn attestation to this truth. If anything has been learned from the failures of previous presidential administrations, it is that frail human beings make mistakes. The ideal American commander-in-chief should be one with the fewest human frailties and weaknesses, augmented by an unquestioned record of moral courage and geopolitical skill.

The senator from New York, lacking in judgement and humility, is not a reassuring prospect for president and commander-in-chief. Her ambition, like the Field of Mars where the Romans offered their sacrifices to the god of war, may prove to be more costly to the American people than their darkest imaginations can fathom.

AMERICA'S CLINTONIAN NIGHTMARE

The lofty tree, under whose shade the nations of the earth had reposed, was deprived of its leaves and branches, and the sapless trunk was left to wither on the ground.

Edward Gibbon, From *The Decline And Fall of the Roman Empire*

If the founding fathers of the American republic could return to Earth and witness the current state of presidential selection in the nation they gave rise to, they would not recognize 21st century America as their creation. It would have been inconceivable to these enlightened political visionaries that, after more than two centuries of political evolution, the United States had reverted to a leadership selection process that bore all the hallmarks of the other nations of the 18th century world, which they saw as so inhumanly flawed.

Though the partisan propagandists of the two dominating political parties in America will spew forth verbal inanities testifying to the vigor of American democracy, the fact that Hillary Rodham Clinton would be perceived and proclaimed as a front-runner presidential candidate is illustrative of the rampant decay within the political processes of the republic. Should she be inaugurated as America's 44th president, it would mean that two families devoid of exceptional virtue or meritorious accomplishment will have had unbroken control of the presidency for possibly seven terms, or 28 years. To the founding fathers, this would signify the end of the American republic and its cherished democratic institutions, as they conceived them at a time when dynastic autocracy ruled much of the world.

George Washington, Thomas Jefferson and the other heroic leaders of the American Revolution would perhaps shed tears of sorrow and distress, perplexed that the United States of the 21st century bore not the least resemblance to the enlightened and virtuous land they had imagined. President Washington, in particular, would be aghast at the contemporary rejection of his admonition to avoid foreign entanglements.

If we look back at the origins of the American republic, it should be recognized that the genius of those who gave birth to America was so powerful, it created institutions and a constitution that withstood a series of mediocre and flawed presidents. What they could not conceive of, however, is that the poisonous alliance of greedy financial interests, and a vulgarized mass media unbeknown to the enlightened 18th century mind, would triangulate with the egotistical and shrill seekers of power who were of a type that were all too familiar to the republic's founders.

King George's tyranny, overthrown by the spirit of 1776, has arisen with vengeance in Washington D.C., in the guise of the Clinton and Bush dynasties. Their triumph has turned the American dream on its head, transforming it into a surreal nightmare.

To the contemporary world, which once looked up to the United States as a role model and beacon of humanity and beneficence, the current state of American political culture has become inexplicable. Having two marginal families monopolize the most powerful political office on Earth, amid the forests of fraud that define the linkage of money with campaign interests that so proliferate the American political landscape, has altered the international perspective of the United States. The American nation is now viewed as having a leadership hierarchy soaked with corruption, and utterly reckless in its dealings with the external world.

The election of Hillary Rodham Clinton as president of the United States, should this in fact occur, will inflict a terminal blow on what still remains of the vitality of the American political experiment. Her inauguration would be perceived as the anointing of a monarch, representative of the egotistical hereditary tyranny over the masses that America's founding fathers revolted against, giving rise to a republic ruled with wisdom and enlightenment. However, Hillary Clinton succeeding George W. Bush, who succeeded her husband, who in turn followed in the footsteps of her predecessor's father, would be a mockery of the nation whose birth is still honored every July 4th.

The broader international community, as well as many among the American people, will correctly view Mrs. Clinton's accession to the White House as a travesty. America's political system will become a point of ridicule, mocked as banal surrealism, an astigmatic distortion of political optics. In essence, Hillary's Clinton's assumption of presidential power will reduce the presidential electoral system of the U.S. into a discordant caricature of itself.

Mass media in the United States has often blurred the lines of demarcation between fantasy and reality. Having the wife of a lecherous and disgraced former president succeed her husband, her succession interrupted by two terms of an inept president who succeeded his father, seems like the discarded script of a mediocre film or single-season television soap opera. Unfortunately, unlike television or cinematic fantasy, the decisions made by the individual who serves as president have enormous consequences, for the world in general and the American people in particular.

In 2008, should the American people be lulled into voting for Hillary Clinton in numbers sufficient for her to claim a majority of the nation's electoral votes, they should be fully aware of the implications of their decision. Far more than voting for a president, they would be casting a ballot for reversing the American Revolution and the enlightened vision of the nation's founding fathers. The culmination of Mrs. Clinton's electoral triumph would be the affirmation that in actuality, if not in name, America has become an imperial entity, having discarded its identity as a republic. The president in reality would be a hereditary monarch, with increasingly authoritarian powers unhindered by a Congress that has consistently displayed is spinelessness, as was the case in surrendering its war making powers on Iraq.

Victory in 2008 for Hillary Clinton, by any measure, will represent an irremediable defeat for the American people. It will bring about a second Clinton presidency, with the disgraced Bill Clinton having another opportunity to wield destructive mayhem on the nation, as the co-president at Hillary's side. The sleaze, perfidious deal-making, cloak and dagger fundraising and outright lies and deception will have their second act, transforming the White House into a true and terrifying theatre of the absurd and ridiculous.

As these pages have outlined and surveyed, viewed on her merits, Hillary Rodham Clinton lacks all the necessary qualities of leadership, skill, knowledge and moral integrity to justify her election as 44th president of the United States. She has only one definite factor, unrelated to her human accoutrements. As the former First Lady, albeit of a disgraceful former president, she has the power of celebrity and name recognition. In the America of 2008, that may very well be all she requires to return to the White House as president and commander-in-chief.

America's manipulated electoral system will reduce the presidential campaign to a reality game show. In effect, voting for the next president will be presented as a popularity contest. To a large extent, the American people will be coaxed into rendering a decision as to which personality they have the strongest affinity towards. Given that all but a handful of voters will have had no personal connection with either Hillary Clinton or her political adversaries, that affinity will be defined largely by thirty second television, radio and Internet sound bites, supplemented with ample quantities of junk mail. Smart and savvy political and media consultants will fabricate some clever phraseology; the candidates will be videotaped repeating the sage words of others as though they were the authentic source of origin, creating plastic images for the American people to pass judgement on.

During the existence of the former Soviet Union, elections were conducted with formalized regularity. Everyone knew they were a sham, and that the official claims of voter approval of the government consistently registering more than 99 percent were fraudulent to the point of being ludicrous. Yet, the Soviet totalitarian state regarded even these sham elections as part of a very important social ritual, in which the people were required to give legitimacy to the imposed ruling class.

America may be a two party state as opposed to single party dominance that characterized Soviet rule. However, the number of striking parallels that are apparent are truly disquieting. American elections have come to resemble the ritualistic carnival campaigns that the Kremlin organized with flourishing pomposity. The large number of American citizens who have chosen not to participate in the voting process would have been most comprehensible to a Soviet citizen who, cynical as he felt, was compelled to "vote" in a meaningless exercise.

The American people have already lost a great deal of confidence in their electoral system. This is a tragedy for the nation, as the lack of faith in American elections translates into a loss of faith in democratic government. Yet, the selfish and egotistical interests that dominate American politics and electoral campaigns are not troubled by the growing alienation of the voters, reflected in plummeting proportions of eligible voters participating in national, state and local elections.

Those in the ruling hierarchies who are not troubled should be. They apparently operate on the assumption that their governing legitimacy is assured, no matter how much of a mockery the contemporary American campaign process has become, especially presidential campaigns. This is a false conviction, and we need only look to the recent demise of the Soviet Union.

The Soviet State did not collapse because of foreign invasion, or a violent civil insurrection. No great natural catastrophe, such as a modern form of the bubonic plague, afflicted the population. In an unprecedented yet defining act of national implosion, the cynicism of the ruled reached a point where the Soviet leaders ceased to have any legitimacy among the people they ruled. Once the population lost complete confidence in the leadership, no manner of carnival election spectaculars could restore it. With the loss of popular legitimacy, the mighty Soviet Union, rival to America as a military and industrial superpower, imploded.

The disintegration of the Soviet Empire through legitimacy-destroying cynicism may be the new paradigm of the 21st century. Indeed, along with the severe external dangers outlined previously, it may be that the growing disenchantment of the American people towards their political rulers comprises one of the most egregious dangers towards the continuity of the American republic.

Hillary Clinton, beyond her personality, is a symbol of the pompous superficiality of the U.S. political establishment that a growing segment of the American population feels so alienated from. Despite the best efforts of the Clintonian public relations machine, too many Americans retain a painful memory of what Hillary Rodham Clinton's husband and political partner wrought on the nation. The behavior of the Clintons during Bill Clinton's two-term presidency, and their mutual political conniving and strategizing since, are beacons of darkness to those who refuse to be charmed by the ritual imitations of Soviet style carnivals.

During the occasion marking the fifth anniversary of the Al-Qaeda atrocities of September 11, 2001 the ABC television network ran a dramatized portrayal of the events leading up to that dark day, "The Road To 9/11." It explored the failures of both the Clinton and Bush administrations that facilitated Al-Qaeda in perpetrating its attacks on the World Trade Center and Pentagon.

In an unprecedented intrusion into the freedom of art and expression in America, and the constitutionally guaranteed right of freedom of speech, ex-president Bill Clinton sought to use his influence to prevent the airing of this television series. He undertook this act of attempted censorship without having seen the television drama, and clearly wanted no American citizens to see it either.

President Clinton claimed that the dramatization of his administration's flawed response was "inaccurate," and that this justified his banal call for banning its broadcast to the American people. However, virtually every politician in America claims that any negative portrayal of them, by whatever medium, lacks objectivity and balance. What is unprecedented with William Jefferson Clinton is that he did not wait for the television series to be broadcast and then issue his critique and condemnation, which he would have been completely entitled to undertake. Instead, the 42nd president of the United States behaved like a Soviet commissar of old, seeking to suppress a point of view on official conduct that was at variance with the Clintonian view of history.

Mr. Clinton's strong-arm tactics in attempting to censure the media are an ominous warning of the true political character of the Clintons. Without question, Bill Clinton took this extraordinary step out of concern for Hillary Clinton as well as his own political legacy. Any reminder of the juxtaposed reality that the president was fornicating and philandering with a White House intern while Osama bin Laden was plotting methodically and tenaciously to assault the American people would clearly prejudice the electoral anointing of the second Clinton presidency. In attempting to stifle free speech and creative expression in America when he thinks it conflicts with his own biased interpretation of history, Bill Clinton has manifested the most sordid and sinister of political rationalizations, that the ends justify the means.

As Bill Clinton's most intimate political collaborator, what reassurance can the American people gleam that Hillary Rodham Clinton does not harbor the same totalitarian inclinations that her husband so wantonly and arrogantly displayed? While her husband was subsumed in exaggerated self-righteous indignation over the public airing of a dramatized television series on one of the most traumatic events in American history, Hillary Clinton was deafeningly silent. Her silence was in reality a decibel-soaring endorsement of Bill Clinton's use of his authority, even diminished in the context of an expired presidency, to censure artistic expression in America.

The desire by Bill Clinton to be the sole judge of what the American people can watch on their television screens when it involves the eight years of his flawed and philandering presidency represents only the most strident form of selective memorization. By presenting to the American people a carefully edited version of the first Clinton presidency, both Bill and Hillary Clinton can publicize a sanitized edition, contrasting it with the ineptitude of George Bush. The objective is clear; manipulate the American electorate into believing that Bill Clinton handed George W. Bush an America at the height of prosperity, security and good governance on a silver platter, and the 43rd president mucked it up. Ipso facto, restoring the Clintons to the White House will restore the happy times of yore.

It is an illusion, constructed on a bedrock of quicksand. Furthermore, a second Clinton presidency is likely to be more cocky and arrogant. The pettiness and moral failures that have already been inflicted on the American people will be revised and updated, fertilized and enhanced by Clintonian contempt. If an out-of-office Clinton would feel no hesitancy in attempting to ban a television broadcast, what might Hillary Clinton, empowered by the presidency, seek to do? These are critical judgements that the American people must deliberate on, unaffected by attempts at clouding the record of the previous Clinton co-presidency.

The flagrant intrusion of President Bill Clinton into the creative decision making process with a major television network suggests a wanton desire to impede the rights of the American people to form their own judgement, be it of history or artistic drama. It is a harbinger of how far the Clintons are prepared to go in their efforts to recapture the White House.

Can America afford a second Clinton presidency? Examining the convergence of discordant economic and geopolitical trends, an objective American voter can only conclude that such a choice would constitute a reckless gamble with the nation's destiny.

After enduring a succession of presidents that were either mediocre or worse, some may conclude that the United States of America is an invincible nation, which shall forever abide no matter how awful the occupant in the White House may be. It is as though many Americans view their nation as a prehistoric reptile, whose armored hide can resist and deflect a shower of spears and arrows for eternity. However, as in the example of the Soviet Union's extirpation, previously cited, such a belief is based purely on myth, and contradicted by the totality of human history.

The Roman Empire, in its time, was believed by its citizens to be a creation of permanence, in spite of a succession of appalling men serving as its imperial rulers. When the English historian, Edward Gibbon, set down his monumental chronicle of the reasons that led to Rome's decline and ultimate fall, paramount among his findings was the cumulative impact of a succession of rotten and egotistically flawed emperors.

The United States at the dawn of the twenty-first century is actually in an unparalleled state of fragility. Its government is financed by an ocean of red ink, with learned economists warning that a day of reckoning will come, made vastly worse by a timid leadership's irrational attempts at continual postponements. Its military, proclaimed as the mightiest in the world, in reality is spread paper-thin, and overwhelmed by a misguided and catastrophic war for which it was never designed. Nuclear proliferation is rife in the most dangerous areas of the world, with only lame verbal responses from American politicians.

At no time in her history was the need for inspired, capable, wise and courageous leadership in Washington D.C. more urgent and compelling. Yet, thus far, the leading candidates of the two main political parties fail to inspire confidence that they have the answers, let alone an honest understanding, to the monumental challenges confronting the United States of American in her third century of existence.

Hillary Rodham Clinton is the most conspicuous example of the failure of American's debilitated political system to cultivate and identify the most capable and qualified American citizens for positions of highest national leadership. What makes her distinct from many of her competitors, but in solidarity with George W. Bush, is that her election would institutionalize a virtual hereditary monarchy as the dominating force in national politics. As we have observed in previous chapters, that in itself would herald a terminal blow at what remains of participatory democracy as the functional means of political succession in the republic.

As the 2008 presidential election looms on the horizon, amid a sea of unimpressive alternatives, Senator Clinton's hopes of emerging as the nation's 44th president depend, to a large extent, on the apathy of the American electorate. If those who go to the polls are, as in previous campaigns, manipulated by media forces and contrived imagery built on a superstructure of superficiality, the odds in favor of Mrs. Clinton's electoral triumph will be significantly enhanced. Her celebrity status and name recognition may prove the most potent dynamics in the upcoming presidential elections.

If, in fact, the American people feel instinctively that crowning a second Clinton as president, following in the wake of the Bush father and son presidencies, is inherently wrong for America, many may still feel perplexed at the paucity of compelling alternatives. Rather than surrender to the inevitability of a fatefully wrong choice for the nation's welfare, perhaps the people of the United States must render a more fundamental choice; rejection of the two mainstream political parties that have jointly led the country along such a calamitous path.

Neither the Democratic nor Republican national parties are owed a permanent right to perpetual two-party dominance of the American republic's governing institutions. Both parties have nominated severely flawed candidates to serve as president and commander-in-chief, as manifested by William Jefferson Clinton and George W. Bush. Should Hillary Rodham Clinton be selected by the Democrats as their presidential standard bearer in 2008, they would be merely replicating sins already egregiously committed by the Republicans. In addition, both mainstream parties have amassed deplorable records of criminal corruption.

A two party political system is only a single party away from absolute dictatorship. Healthy democracies have multiple mainstream parties, typically three or four. Especially in Western Europe, it is not unusual for two or more political parties to form a coalition government after an election, if there is no decisive winner. In times past, America has had viable third parties. In 1912, a former president. Theodore Roosevelt left the Republican Party to run for the Bull Moose Party under a reformist political platform.

In contemporary America, the only recent example of a viable third party alternative involved a wealthy entrepreneur, who could use his vast financial resources to buy media time and visibility. That is not an ultimate prescription to America's need for an effective alternative to the current two-party dictatorship.

With the emergence of new technologies that empower the common citizen, especially Internet based community and political blogs, an opportunity exists for the multitudes to link together, and build their own grass-roots political movement. The initial goal should not be to endorse a particular ideology of the right or left, but rather to mobilize the vast majority of Americans of either persuasion who manifest decency and common sense, and who have an innate awareness that a critical affliction has gripped the mainstream political parties. A virtual third party structure can thereby be created, with one overriding objective. The task of a Internet based new political party would be to identify the American men and women most qualified to provide the excellence in leadership so urgently required for national survival and renewal.

Rather than have egotistical politicians campaign for nomination, only those *not* seeking office would be considered. Through the Internet, broadly based citizens committees could be formed, which would research and identify those who merit consideration, from segments of the population normally excluded from consideration from presidential office. For too long, the legal profession has dominated the presidential nominating process of the two monopolizing parties at all electoral levels, including the presidency. The grass-roots nominating and search committees would break the hegemony of the lawyers, and look at categories such as educators, small business owners of exemplary record and highly successful entrepreneurs of exceptional merit, farmers, journalists, health care providers and the scientific community. A list of possibilities that would be automatically *excluded* by both the Democratic and Republican parties, but which would open up a radically refreshing pool of human potential, reflective of the true ingenuity and capability of the American people, would be created.

Contrast the megalomaniac pursuit of presidential power by Hillary Clinton with the record of Bill Gates. Having founded Microsoft, and created a product that revolutionized the world, he could have chosen a life of perpetual leisure. He also could have mimicked other affluent Americans, and use his financial resources to "buy" himself political office by funding his own election campaign. Mr. Gates instead chose a path that demonstrates true leadership is an expression of personal commitment, modesty and generosity, as opposed to the egotistical acquisition of power. Choosing to surrender his business interests while at his peak, Bill Gates decided to devote his time and financial resources to alleviating poverty and illness while enhancing education, throughout the world.

Would not a person of Bill Gate's qualities, problem-solving skills and visionary aptitude be vastly more qualified for presidential leadership than Hillary Rodham Clinton or her ilk? Would not his proven record of service to humanity, and real world achievements in revolutionizing technology throughout the world, be more inspiring to the American people than Mrs. Clinton's turgid recitation of vapid speeches written by others?

Mr. Gates is only one of a large number of exceptional American men and women who have chosen not to become professional politicians, but who are infinitely more capable of providing the caliber of leadership America needs than the apoplectic range of mediocre offerings that dominate the choices being presented by the Democrats and Republicans.

A system that offered a true electoral choice to the American people would run counter to the narrow interests of the two dominating political parties, and the special interests and lobbyists that profit from their political monopoly on government in the Unites States. It can be expected that the leadership of the Republican and Democratic parties will do everything in their power to thwart any popular grassroots movement which seeks to offer the American people a real and more worthy alternative to succeed President Bush.

However, many sincere adherents of both parties instinctively recognize that the two party system has failed the American people. Grass roots Republicans and Democrats who put country ahead of partisanship can play a decisive role in cleansing the body politic, and putting the nation back on the right track towards solvency and sanity. A popularly constructed third party presidential win in 2008 would compel the Republicans and Democrats to purge their ranks of the egotistical, inept and corrupt, and rebuild themselves into entities that honestly and capably represent their divergent ideological perspectives. Ultimately, a viable three party political structure would enhance American democracy, and strengthen the republic. It would also attract a new generation of leaders, representing a vastly improved selection of electoral candidates, devoid of the celebrity syndrome that has rendered contemporary American politics so egregiously dysfunctional.

Absent a credible third party alternative, Hillary Clinton enjoys favorable odds of becoming America's 44th president. There are primarily two reasons that underscore her electoral viability.

Among the recognized contenders for the Democratic Party's presidential nomination, Senator Clinton enjoys by far the greatest name recognition, due to her celebrity status and similar factors identified in earlier chapters. The visible and subtle forms of support her political partner and husband will render her will be of inestimable value, unmatched by any of her opponents.

Having secured her party's nomination, Mrs. Clinton will then have the enviable task of running against the record of George W. Bush, even though the 43rd president will not have his name on the ballot. Any likely Republican presidential nominee will carry the burden of George Bush's failed legacy of ineptitude as Christ carried the cross to his crucifixion at Calvary. American political history provides many sobering examples where the electorate chose a candidate that it was unenthusiastic about, because it wished to vote against the incumbent's record. Too many Americans harbor negative feelings towards the two terms of Bush to grant consideration to his party's chosen successor, no matter what his or her merits may be. The example of Al Gore paying for the sins of Bill Clinton is only a recent example of this recurring political phenomenon.

Given the torrent of favorable forces propelling a Hillary Clinton presidential campaign towards its ultimate goal, only the complacent among those who understand the dark implications of such an outcome would write off her chances of becoming the nation's next president.

If Hillary Rodham Clinton, come January 2009, is inaugurated as the 44th president, it will mark a chilling and uncertain chapter in the annals of American history. As this writer has elaborated on throughout this book, a convergence of geopolitical and economic forces will intersect during the next president's term of office, creating a vortex that may rip the very roots out of the foundations that constitute the republic. The debilitating flaws of ego and avariciousness that characterize Hillary Rodham Clinton, magnified by the corrosive influence of William Jefferson Clinton, will render her insufficient, to put it mildly, to navigate the American ship of state through the stormy waters that await.

A Clintonian nightmare beckons the people of the United States. The corrupting lust for power manifested in both Hillary and Bill Clinton threatens to unleash the emergence of a period of nocturnal darkness for the nation, suffocating its viability and perhaps its very existence. In the 2008 presidential election, nothing less than the very survival of the American republic, conceived as a land based on constitutional liberty, is at stake. All the distortions of political corruption, lobbyist influence, ineptitude and megalomania threaten the imposition of dynastic rule in America. Only the aroused common sense of the American people and their collective wisdom and fortitude can defeat the imposition of the inherently un-American concept of family dynastic rule in Washington.

Should the American people in their righteousness render a decision in 2008 that reverses the pattern of the past 20 years, renewal and revival await a long-suffering nation.

If, however, the people fail to exercise their constitutional and civic duty at the ballot boxes with discretion and wisdom, thus allowing Hillary Rodham Clinton to triumph, only ruination and national demise can follow in her wake.

Printed in the United States
105446LV00002B/155/A

9 781425 967598